CROSS PURPOSES

DISCOVERING THE
GREAT LOVE OF GOD *for* YOU

D. JAMES KENNEDY
& JERRY NEWCOMBE

Multnomah Publishers

CROSS PURPOSES
published by Multnomah Publishers
A division of Random House Inc.

Published in association with
William K. Jensen Literary Agency, Eugene, Oregon.
© 2007 by D. James Kennedy and Jerry Newcombe
International Standard Book Number: 1-59052-969-3

Cover design by Studiogearbox.com
Interior design and tyeset by Katherine Lloyd, The DESK, Sisters, OR

Italics in Scripture quotations are the authors' emphasis.
Unless otherwise indicated, Scripture quotations are from:
The Holy Bible, New King James Version (NKJV)
© 1984 by Thomas Nelson, Inc.

Also quoted:
The Holy Bible, *English Standard Version* (ESV) © 2001 by Crossway Bibles,
a division of Good News Publishers.Used by permission. All rights reserved.
The Holy Bible, King James Version (KJV)
The Holy Bible, New International Version (NIV) © 1973, 1984 by International
Bible Society, used by permission of Zondervan Publishing House

Multnomah is a trademark of Multnomah Publishers
and is registered in the U.S. Patent and Trademark Office.
The colophon is a trademark of Multnomah Publishers.

Printed in the United States of America

For information:
MULTNOMAH PUBLISHERS
12265 Oracle Boulevard, Suite 200
Colorado Springs, Colorado 80921

Library of Congress Cataloging-in-Publication Data
Kennedy, D. James (Dennis James), 1930-
Cross purposes : discovering the great love of God for you / D. James Kennedy
and Jerry Newcombe.
    p. cm.
"Published in association with William K. Jensen Literary Agency, Eugene, Oregon".
Includes index.
ISBN 1-59052-969-3
1. God--Love. I. Newcombe, Jerry. II. Title.
BT140.K465 2007
231'.6--dc22   2006032620
07 08 09 10 11 12—10 9 8 7 6 5 4 3 2 1 0

This book is dedicated to the memory of
Charlie Hainline,
long time active lay evangelist in our church,
who never failed to proclaim the message of the cross
to anyone who would listen.

Other Books by D. JAMES KENNEDY:

Beginning Again

Character & Destiny

Christ's Passion

Delighting God

Evangelism Explosion

The Gates of Hell Shall Not Prevail

Help, God, I Hurt!

How Do I Live for God?

Foundations for Your Faith

Led by the Carpenter

Lord of All

Messiah: Prophecies Fulfilled

New Every Morning

Secrets of Successful Marriage

Skeptics Answered

The Da Vinci Myth Versus the Gospel Truth

The Real Meaning of the Zodiac

The Secret to a Happy Home

Solving Bible Mysteries

Truth for Lies

Truths That Transform

Turn It to Gold

What If America Were a Christian Nation Again?

What If Jesus Had Never Been Born?

What If the Bible Had Never Been Written?

What's Wrong with Same-Sex Marriage?

Why I Believe

Why the Ten Commandments Matter

The Wolves Among Us

CONTENTS

DISCOVER
THE ESSENCE

God is love.
1 JOHN 4:8

O nce upon a time, there was a young prince who was set to marry a beautiful princess. But something happened— a wicked serpent entered the picture and deceived the princess and made her unacceptable to the prince. Yet the prince still loved her, and he left the glories of his father's palace to win her back. He gave his own life on behalf of the princess, who had now become ugly from following the serpent's way. The prince, however, was raised back to life by his father. Because of his love for her, the prince made the unlovely and unacceptable princess lovely once again. They were married, and they lived happily ever after. The end.

Dr. Warren Gage, professor at Knox Theological Seminary, notes that fairy tales like the above composite sketch are all reflective of the Christian gospel. The Bible begins with a wedding (that of Adam and Eve), and it ends with a wedding (the marriage feast of the Lamb, wherein Christ metaphorically weds His bride, the church—all those who have truly put their faith in Him).

So great is the love of God that when we lost our way because of our sin in following the serpent, He sent His one and only Son, and He Himself paid that which He did not owe to win us back. He paid a debt for us that was so great we could never pay for it ourselves.

This book is dedicated to exploring the magnificent truths of the cross of Jesus Christ. Here are four dozen meditations to help you consider various aspects of the awful price Jesus Christ paid for us when He suffered death for us—even death on a cross.

Each meditation includes a Scripture verse at the beginning and a quotation near the end. The final thought we leave you with in each meditation is the beginning of a prayer; our hope is that this will be the springboard for your own prayer of thanksgiving for what Christ has accomplished on the cross. (This is why we don't end these prayers as we normally would: "In Jesus' name. Amen.")

This book may be used for your personal devotion or for corporate devotion. The goal of each short chapter is to discover afresh the great love God has for you—the essence of which is Christ crucified for your sake and mine.

1

THE RICHES
OF HIS GRACE

That in the ages to come He might show the exceeding riches
of His grace in His kindness toward us in Christ Jesus.

EPHESIANS 2:7

Amazing grace—how sweet the sound. The more I think about it, the more convinced I am that grace is the greatest thought to ever enter the mind of man. Grace encapsulates in one word the essence of the Christian gospel.

This amazing grace of which we sing is what we are saved by. We are saved, we are redeemed, we are taken to heaven, we enjoy paradise, we avoid the pains of hell—all by *grace*. Therefore, it is a term of exceeding importance, is it not? And yet I've discovered, over many years of talking to many people, that the meaning of grace isn't clear. I've yet to meet one unconverted person who could tell me what it was—could define it or even come close to defining it.

Now, if it is true that we're saved by grace, then it's important to ask ourselves: Can we define it? And if it is true, as I suppose, that no unconverted person can tell me what it is, I think it would be important to *you* to make sure *you* can define it.

Think for a moment. Grace is _____. What? Your answer to that question may reveal where you really stand with God.

Did you answer it? Do you know what this marvelous term means?

We may be able to define it some way, but one thing is certain: We can never comprehend it, because it plumbs the profoundest depths of human thought. It scales the dizziest heights of divine revelation. And though we may get ahold of a little corner of it, we can never fully comprehend it with our minds. It is, indeed, beyond full comprehension; it is the greatest thought in all the world.

In the Greek language, the word is *charis*—a lovely term. And what does it mean—this beautiful word?

Many people suppose that grace is essentially justice. Since the Bible says we are saved "by grace" (Ephesians 2:8), and since they believe we're saved by living a good life and following the Ten Commandments and keeping the Golden Rule and doing the best we can, they suppose grace is another word for fairness. It is a *quid pro quo*—do this and you get that, tit for tat, perfect equity. They think this is what grace is really all about: If I do the best I can and try to live a good life, then I certainly ought to go to heaven, and if I don't get to heaven, then that just wouldn't be fair.

The first thing you need to know about the Christian gospel is that it isn't fair. Be glad it isn't! Since all of us deserve hell, fairness would mean that hell is where we all would go. So thank God, the gospel is not fair.

Ordinarily when we say something isn't fair, we mean it's *less* than fair. Let's say you work at a job making ten dollars an hour. After a forty-hour week, your paycheck should be $400.

And if you get $400, that would be fair; it would be equity; it would be proper.

But suppose your boss gives you only $295. You would go and tell him, "This isn't fair."

On the other hand, suppose after another forty-hour week you get a paycheck made out for ten million dollars. Again you tell your boss, "This isn't fair"—but this time you mean that it's more than fair; it's wonderfully not fair.

That's exactly what the gospel is—wonderfully more than fair. It is not a *quid pro quo*, tit for tat, this for that kind of a thing.

The full meaning of grace is seen in the cross. Because of my sin, justice demands that I experience the wrath of God. Instead, because of grace, God has taken all my slimy iniquity

"Grace flows from His very nature. It was made available to us even when we were dead in our trespasses and sin." (Ken Hemphill)

and placed it on His own Son. And the just anger of God has fallen upon *Him*, and Jesus in His own spirit and soul and body has borne the penalty for all our iniquity and cried out, "It is done. It is finished. It is paid. It is enough!" He has buried our sins beneath the depths of the sea. He has placed them as far from us as the east is from the west, never to remember them against us.

So rich is the love of God for us. This love is best seen in His Son suffering on the cross in our place.

The whole world without Christ is lost. He comes with infinite mercy and condescension, with the exceeding riches of His grace, willing to forgive us and cleanse us from every spot of sin. He comes to make us whiter than snow, to clothe us in the righteousness of His own Son, to adopt us into His family, to pardon and justify us, to make us His heir, and to provide for us and take us at last into mansions of paradise. This is only the hem of the garment of the exceeding riches of His grace.

Prayer: Father, thank You for Your grace poured out on us by Your Spirit because of Your Son's death for us on the cross.

"We who live on this side of the Cross have no reason to ever doubt that God loves us." (Anonymous)

2

WHAT IS GRACE?

For by grace you have been saved through faith.
EPHESIANS 2:8

We saw in the previous chapter that grace is something unearned and undeserved; we saw what grace is *not*. Now we want to see what grace *is*.

Many years ago, I read a story that deeply touched me and that says something about the meaning of grace. The story takes us back to the middle of the nineteenth century, out in the hinterlands of czarist Russia.

Imagine that you are looking across a vast panorama of the frozen white steppes of Russia. You focus in closer, and you see a dogsled traveling across those vast expanses of ice. And if you get close enough, you'll observe a Russian nobleman seated on the sled, while holding the reins is an older man—the nobleman's faithful servant of many years.

These two have been traveling for several hundred miles on their way home, and now, at last, their destination is only about twenty miles ahead. They're rejoicing at the prospect of a warm bed and hot food.

As he drives the dogs, the servant has been examining the horizon all around, and now, as he takes a look back, he notices a large dark mass about a mile or so behind them. As he peers closer, he sees a sight that freezes his blood. He realizes a horde of wolves has caught their scent and is now inexorably closing in upon the dogsled.

13

He gives the reins to the dogs, snaps the whip, and cries the Russian equivalent of "Mush!" The dogs lean into the harness to make as much speed as they can. Still, the pack of wolves draws closer. Now they're but a half mile away...a quarter mile...a few hundred yards...fifty yards...ten...five.

The wolves are now right behind them! The two men can hear their heavy breathing; the creatures' red eyes seem like red-hot coals from the very pit of hell. Their yellow fangs are dripping with saliva in anticipation of their next meal.

There's no place to hide, no place else to go; the men and the dogs cannot outrun these wolves. Their situation is hopeless.

Suddenly, unexpectedly, this old servant throws himself backward off the dogsled—with predictable results. The wolf pack stops and converges on the old servant...while his master is spared.

GRACE = God's Riches At Christ's Expense.

When I first read that story, I said to myself, "That is grace." On more mature reflection, I realized this story is but the foothills of grace. It does at least bring out one aspect, one facet of this precious diamond of grace—that grace involves a great sacrifice, even the sacrifice of one's own life for another.

But to understand even further the amazing grace of God, let's suppose the nobleman in that story had repeatedly abused his servant, physically and emotionally. In this light, the servant's sacrifice would be even greater.

Or what if we change up the story even more? What if the servant hadn't really been faithful after all, but had always been lazy, mean-spirited, and disrespectful—and it was then the *nobleman* who threw himself to the wolves to save the other man's life? This, too, would be a picture of God's grace toward us.

The Bible declares: "God demonstrates His own love toward

us, in that while we were still sinners, Christ died for us" (Romans 5:8).

We're all guilty of killing the Son of God. Grace involves unmerited favor to the wickedest of sinners. It doesn't matter how bad you've been; in the words of a well-known hymn (which paraphrases Scripture), we have received "grace greater than all our sin." How big your sin is doesn't matter; grace is greater. "Where sin abounded, grace abounded much more" (Romans 5:20). Grace is greater than all the sin of all the world. This is the grace that saves us. "For by grace you have been saved through faith, and that not of yourselves; it is the gift of God, not of works, lest anyone should boast" (Ephesians 2:8–9).

Prayer: Dear Father, thank You for the amazing grace made available through Your Son.

"Grace comes into the soul, as the morning sun into the world, first a dawning; then a light; and at last the sun in his full and excellent brightness." (Thomas Adams)

HOW TO GET RIGHT WITH GOD

*But as many as received Him, to them He gave the right
to become children of God, to those who believe in His name.*

JOHN 1:12

When God created humankind, all was well and right with the world. Humanity's relationships with God were pure and unbroken. But when Satan deceived Adam and Eve, those relationships were broken. And ever since, man has been striving to get right with God again.

How do we get right with God? And what does the cross have to do with it?

Getting right with God is by faith in Jesus Christ and not by works. This faith, if it is true faith, will result in good works. But we're not saved by doing good works.

The apostle Paul declared, "A man is not justified by the works of the law but by faith in Jesus Christ"; we believe in Jesus "that we might be justified by faith in Christ and not by the works of the law; for by the works of the law no flesh shall be justified" (Galatians 2:16).

We cannot add to what Christ did on the cross. When Jesus died, He declared, "It is finished" (John 19:30). We cannot add in any way to this finished work on the cross.

I remember a story about some people who moved into a new house, and they had a good friend who was a German woodworker, a master craftsman. He was invited to see the house, and as he looked around it he noticed that there was no coffee table in the living room.

He never said anything, but after he left he started to work in his workshop, and he worked for two months. He built the most magnificent coffee table imaginable, with the most gorgeous curved legs and all kinds of various designs in it. He put sixteen coats of varnish on the surface until it became a veritable mirror.

Finally, he wrapped it in a soft cloth and brought it over to their house, set it down in the living room, threw off the cloth, and said, "Voilà!" There it was.

"Ahhhhh…beautiful!" It was, without a doubt, the most beautiful table they had ever seen in their lives.

Then the craftsman said, "You are my dearest friends, and I present this to you as a gift."

The man of the house then stepped out of the living room and came back in a moment with a piece of course sandpaper in his hand. He said to the craftsman, "Oh, thank you again for your gift. And now I must do my part."

"Don't touch that!" the craftsman said. "If you touch it, you'll ruin it. It is already finished. It is complete. It is done!"

Likewise we read that Jesus said on the cross, "It is finished." It is complete. It is done. It is perfect. As the hymn says, "Jesus paid it all. All to Him I owe."

So I ask you: Have you received this perfect gift of eternal life? Have you trusted in Christ alone as your only hope of eternal life? Have you trusted in His finished work on the cross alone for the salvation of your soul?

DID YOU KNOW?
When Jesus hung on the cross and had finished paying for our sins, He declared, "It is finished." The Greek word there is *tetelestai*—a financial term meaning "paid in full." Christ paid for our sins in full.

Throw the sandpaper away. There is nothing more that needs to be done for your salvation. And even if there were, there's nothing *you* could do. It is Christ alone who makes us right with God.

Prayer [If you have not put your faith solely in Christ's finished work on the cross, please consider praying along these lines]: *Lord Jesus Christ, come into my heart. Cleanse me. Forgive me. Justify me by Your grace because of Your death upon the cross. I abandon all trust in any goodness of my own and place my trust in You only, and I turn away from my sins and ask You to take control of my life and help me to follow You. Thank You right now for the gift of eternal life. In Your name, amen.*

"Nothing in my hands I bring.
Simply to the cross I cling."
(Augustus M. Toplady)

❦

4

BLESSED ASSURANCE

These things have I written to you who believe
in the name of the Son of God, that you may know that
you have eternal life, and that you may continue
to believe in the name of the Son of God.

1 JOHN 5:13

Not long ago a radio announcer in Chicago took a survey in a train station. He asked about twenty-five or thirty people this question: "Do you know for sure that you're going to go to heaven when you leave this world?"

The result was interesting. There was a unanimous response; they all said no. In fact, one or two even became indignant, and several said, "Why, nobody could know such a thing as that. The very idea!"

Contrast this reaction, if you would, with the fact that many people in past generations knew they were going to heaven. The great scientist Sir Michael Faraday, the distinguished nineteenth-century pioneer of electromagnetism, was also a great Christian. When he was asked on his deathbed, "Sir Michael, what speculations do you have about life after death?" he replied in astonishment. "Speculations? Why I have no speculations. I'm resting on certainties. I know whom I have believed, and am persuaded that He is able to keep that which I have committed unto Him against that day."

Such assurance was a possession of not only the great and

wise of the world, but also of the poor and humble. I think of the story of an elderly Scottish woman who lay at death's door. Her pastor came to see her, and as was the custom, he inquired into the reality of her faith, probing deeply. At last, he asked her this penetrating question: "Sadie, after all God has done for you, suppose that when you die, He still allows you to perish. What then?"

Sadie answered, "Well, that's up to Him. He will do what He will. However, if He does allow me to perish, then He will lose more than I, for though I will lose my soul, He will lose His honor, for He has promised me in His Word, 'He that trusteth in Me shall never perish.'"

Indeed, it would be strange if God would put into a person's heart the assurance of going to heaven when, in fact, that person was hastening into hell.

In that Chicago train station referred to on the previous page, the people participating in that survey were all assuming that their entry into heaven would be based on their own efforts, their own striving, their own churchgoing, their own goodness, their own character, their own morality, their own commandment-keeping. (And they were honest enough to see their shortcomings in those areas.)

Assurance of salvation can lead to great joy. The great scientist Blaise Pascal was also a devout Christian who was converted to Christ in 1654. He wrote on a piece of parchment his feelings of the experience of salvation: "Joy, joy, joy, tears of joy." Os Guinness notes: "This testimony was found sewn into his clothing after his death. It appears that he carried it with him at all times."

But basing our hope of heaven on such things is the very antithesis of Christianity. No wonder these people couldn't *know* they were going to heaven; no wonder they lacked assurance.

Likewise, the reason so many in the church today fail to *know* they're going to heaven is simply that they are *not* going to heaven. It's generally true that all who *are* going to heaven know that they are.

But sometimes there's a situation with a sensitive soul who has come to faith in Christ, but who still is not quite so sure of his or her salvation. The great news for such a person is that we *can* be sure. As Jesus said, "He who believes in Me *has* everlasting life" (John 6:47).

Assurance of salvation is the wellspring of all Christian motives for holy living. Unless you know you have eternal life, everything you've ever done for Christ is a sin.

I'll say it again: Unless *you know* you have eternal life, everything you've done for Christ has been a sin—because your motive was wrong. If you don't know you have eternal life, everything you're doing is an effort to *get* eternal life, and thus your motive is gain and greed instead of thanksgiving.

However, God in His mercy comes down, incarnate in Christ, dies on the cross, and pays for our sins. He purchases for us eternal life and by His graciousness offers it freely to us as a gift. Faith is but the hand of a beggar reaching out to receive the gift of a King. In such a relationship, the motive for Christian living is not gain, but gratitude for the gift of eternal life.

When we've accepted the gift of eternal life, we can sing with confidence: "Blessed assurance, Jesus is mine, oh what a foretaste of glory divine!" Amen.

Prayer: Dear Father, thank You for giving us
Your Spirit that we may know we have eternal life
through Jesus Christ our Lord.

"Perfect submission, all is at rest.
I in my Savior am happy and blessed."
(Fanny Crosby)

5

WE'RE NO ANGELS

For all have sinned and fall short of the glory of God.

ROMANS 3:23

There are three key ingredients that led to the cross. We'll look at them in three chapters, beginning with this one.

The first key ingredient to Calvary is mankind's sin.

Without sin there would be no need for Calvary. There would never have been a cross with anybody on it—much less the Son of God—were it not for the sin of mankind. And yet, amazingly, people today have increasingly lost sight of the reality of sin.

Dr. Karl Menninger, head of the Menninger Clinic and famed psychiatrist, wrote a notable book some years ago entitled *Whatever Became of Sin?* Indeed, whatever happened to sin? It seems to have disappeared, doesn't it? You could spend a year watching all the soap operas each morning (if you do, may God help you) and all the talk shows each afternoon (if you do, you'll need God's help even more) and probably never hear the word *sin*.

Whatever happened to sin?

22

People have the general idea that they're good. I've even occasionally run into somebody who supposes that everybody is good, and that there's really no such thing as a bad person or a sinful person—that sin doesn't really exist. It's merely a fiction invented by preachers to make people feel bad. Have these people ever read the front page of the newspaper?

I remember talking to such a couple one time and saying to them, "I wonder if I may see your keys. Do you have a key ring?"

The man reached in his pocket and pulled out his key ring.

I said to him, "If there's no such thing as sin, sir, tell me, why do you have these?"

He was speechless. He has keys because he has locks. And why does he have locks? Because he has things locked up. And why does he have things locked up? Because there are people who would steal them if he didn't. And why would they steal them? Because they're sinners. That's why.

Let me assure you of something. You'll never ever, ever, ever hear the sound of keys in heaven. There are no keys in heaven because there are no locks and no locks because there are no sinners in heaven. (God changes believers instantly upon death in a process called glorification. We will instantly become sinless—incapable of committing sin.)

> God does not grade on the curve. The passing grade for entry into heaven is like everything else there—perfection. Jesus said it clearly: "Therefore you shall be perfect, just as your Father in heaven is perfect" (Matthew 5:48).

Here on earth, I'm afraid we're all sinners. The Bible says:

- "There is not a just man on earth who does good and does not sin" (Ecclesiastes 7:20).
- "The heart is deceitful above all things, and desperately wicked" (Jeremiah 17:9).

- "There is none righteous, no, not one.... There is none who seeks after God. They have all turned aside.... There is none who does good, no, not one.... Their feet are swift to shed blood; destruction and misery are in their ways.... There is no fear of God before their eyes" (Romans 3:10–18).

We are a fallen race, and because we are fallen, we are condemned: Christ said, "He who does not believe is condemned already" (John 3:18).

How terrible is sin? We haven't a clue. We live in it. We wallow in it. It's up to our necks. Only those who live in a perfect world like heaven would have the foggiest notion of how horrific sin really is. Sin is everything that's against God's law and God's will.

This terrible thing called sin inevitably draws upon itself the wrath of God. May we never forget that though we may become ever so complacent in the face of sin, and so accepting of it, God is infinitely holy and has an infinite hatred for sin. He is of purer eyes than even to look upon iniquity. And He has promised that He will visit our transgressions with the rod and that His wrath will inevitably fall upon our sins. This includes all of us, since we've all broken His law in words and thoughts and deeds.

But Christ took on our sin for our sake. Our sins nailed Him to that cross.

Prayer: Merciful Father, when I see your Son scourged and crowned with piercing thorns, when I see Him languishing on the cross, please let me remember it was my sins that brought Him to such a place.

"The chief problem in America today is not getting people saved. It is getting people to realize they are lost."
(Lay evangelist Charlie Hainline)

THE JUSTICE
OF GOD

The LORD will not leave the guilty unpunished.
NAHUM 1:3, NIV

We have seen that our sin is the first ingredient that put Christ on the cross. The second ingredient that went into making Calvary is *the justice of God*.

Now justice, by definition, is where righteousness is rewarded and sin, or evil, is punished. God must do that. He has sworn that He will. He says, "Then will I visit their transgression with the rod, and their iniquity with stripes" (Psalm 89:32, KJV).

Therefore God must be just. Should He fail to punish any sin, God would be ripped from His throne and cast into the mire and mud with the rest of us sinners. But God will not be unjust, though many people want Him to simply overlook their sin. (Actually, they don't see themselves as God sees them. In their natural states, they see themselves as good, but God sees all their sins.)

That presents a problem, doesn't it? If you take the sin of man and the justice of God and bring them together, you'll inevitably produce hell. Nothing else can come out of that combination.

When I was in seminary, I went to a jail to preach the gospel to those who were locked up inside. I had never been to a place like that to preach, and I must say I was a little unnerved by it. I was sent into a big room where I was separated by bars from probably a dozen prisoners. As they were milling around, I started to talk to them. I probably hadn't gotten two minutes into my talk when one of the largest inmates suddenly came at the bars (which I was happy were there at that point) and said to me, "Mister, you just go tell that God of yours all I want from Him is what I deserve!"

"Sir," I replied, "if you got what you deserved from God, the floor would open up right where you stand and drop you straight into hell, for that is precisely what you deserve. I don't say that because you're behind these bars while I'm outside them, because that is what we all deserve. If we got our just deserts, we would each and every one be condemned—because, you see, we're actually already condemned. Christ said of the whole human race, 'You are condemned already.'"

We're not sitting on a fence; we're not in neutral ground. We are *condemned already.* "He who does not believe is condemned already, because he has not believed in the name of the only begotten Son of God" (John 3:18).

The great Reformer John Calvin declared that God gave us His law to show us our need for His salvation: "The law was given in order to convert a great into a little man—to show that you have no power of your own for righteousness; and might thus, poor, needy, and destitute, flee to grace."

We are sinners, criminals before the bar of justice, waiting for the execution of the sentence of death and hell. Into this black background of sin and death, God sent His Son so that we might not perish, but have everlasting life.

That is the greatest story ever told. It's the story of the incarnation of the love of God. That's why the gospel is not fair; it is *beyond* fair.

Perhaps you've heard the statement: "Good people go to heaven, and bad people go to hell." I remember one time when somebody said that to me, and I replied, "No, that is not the way it goes."

He said, "Well, if it doesn't go that way, it's just not fair."

Someone else said to me, "What's wrong with the idea that good people go to heaven and the bad people go to hell?"

"I'll tell you," I answered. "The problem is the fact that there are no good people."

In the last chapter we saw several Scriptures—statement after statement—showing how we're all sinners. With that in mind, let's examine the thesis that good people go to heaven and bad people go to hell. If you aren't good, you're bad, and if there is none good—no, not one—then where is *everybody* in the world going to end up? You've got it. In hell, which is where we belong. It's what we deserve. And that is the problem.

God hates sin. He will punish sin. I would remind you of one inescapable fact, and there is no possible way around it: Every sin you've ever committed will be visited by the infinite wrath of God—a God who hates sin with an infinite hatred. You cannot escape it. The only question is whether this wrath will meet that sin when it is on you...or when it is on Christ on the cross. But your sin shall meet the wrath of God. I guarantee that.

The justice of God is seen at the cross because God will not just "overlook" sin. He will punish it, one way or the other.

---

*Prayer: God of justice, we tremble at Your holiness—
especially in light of our sin. Thank You, Jesus,
for paying the penalty we justly deserve for our sins.*

"The squirrel in his wire cage continually in motion but making no progress reminds me of my own self-righteous efforts toward salvation." (Charles Spurgeon)

THE LOVE OF GOD

Your mercy, O LORD, is in the heavens; Your faithfulness reaches to the clouds. Your righteousness is like the great mountains; Your judgments are a great deep.

PSALM 36:5–6

We have seen God's justice, our sin, and the fact that we stand condemned already. But God doesn't leave us there. He makes a way out.

It takes something far greater than justice for us to escape hell in the afterlife. It takes the incredible, amazing, unfathomable *love of God*, which changes hell into Calvary. The love of God produced the cross.

I've told my congregation at Coral Ridge Presbyterian Church in Ft. Lauderdale that if there were some local disaster of some kind—a fire or a flood or something similar—I hope I would be willing to give my life to save them. And I hope and trust that every Christian man and woman would be courageous enough to do the same.

But I can tell you without a doubt that there isn't one person in our congregation whom I would save if it meant losing the life of my daughter. And I have a feeling that everyone reading this book shares that sentiment about his or her own family.

And yet, God *so* loved the world that *He gave His only begotten Son.* Wonder of wonders that the Creator would die for the creatures' sin. How astonishing that Jesus, there on the cross, would pray for those who had just nailed Him to that horrible cross.

The cross is powerful. The cross is at the heart of the gospel, which Paul tells us is the "power of God" (Romans 1:16). The Greek word used there is *dynamos*, from which we get the word *dynamite*. The gospel of the cross of Christ is the dynamite of God.

This truth is encapsulated well in one verse. John 3:16 is like the Bible in a nutshell, the whole essence of Christianity wrapped up in one verse.

In the English text, of course, the verse begins, "For God so loved the world," but not so in the Greek text. There it begins with the biggest small word, or the smallest big word, in the Bible. It's the word *so*, and it is placed in the emphatic position. We could translate it: "*Thus* God loved the world that He gave His only Son."

In the Old Testament there were glimmerings of the fact that God loved at least the Israelites. They believed God's love was their personal possession, and it belonged only to them. Likewise the Messiah would be theirs alone, and no one else's. Gentiles were but dogs—of no value—and there was no measure of God's love given to them.

> "Could we with ink the ocean fill
> And were the skies of parchment made,
> Were ev'ry stalk on earth a quill,
> And every man a scribe by trade,
> To write the love of God above
> Would drain the ocean dry.
> Nor could the scroll contain the whole,
> Tho' stretched from sky to sky."
> (Frederick M. Lehman)

But now, here it is—the simple word *so*, a simple single-syllable word: "God *so* loved the world." That is the whole emphasis of the verse.

I remember seeing a line of eensy, weensy, teensy sugar ants in one of our rooms at home, and I watched them with some interest to see just where they were going. They all went the same way, and they were so tiny I couldn't see any particular part moving, but I watched them cross the floor. I wonder what you would think if I declared, "I love those ants." You would think I lost my mind.

Or, even more, what if I said, "I love them so much, I'm going to give my daughter to die for them."

May I point out to you, there is a far greater gulf between God and us than there is between us and those ants—even the tiniest of them. Of course, I didn't create those ants, but God created us. You see now something of God's incredible love—that He would love *us*.

Let us imagine that these ants were vicious, and in great swarms they would come upon people in their sleep and mutilate and kill them. Should I love them now? Rather, I would have a debugging tent over my house before you could say Jack Robinson, and I would exterminate every one of them. Yet God *loves* sinners such as we are. These are the people He loves. Not only do we have no comprehension of the real greatness of God; we have no comprehension of the extent of our sin.

So you take the sin of men and the justice of God and add to that the infinite love of God, and you produce Calvary and the salvation of man. What a wondrous thing it is.

May I point out to you that should you travel the whole world and visit every town and city on this earth and explore every religion on this planet, you will never read or hear a message like this other than from Christians. For no one else died for your sins but Christ. No one else made an atonement to reconcile you to God. Christ came that we might have life in Him and have it abundantly.

Prayer: Father, by Your Spirit, show us Your
love and Your grace made available
through the cross of Your dear Son.

"He gave his own son as a ransom for us: the holy for the unholy, the innocent for the sinners, the righteous for the unjust, the incorruptible for the corruptible, and the immortal for the mortal." (Justin Martyr)

❧

8

THE GREAT BARRIER
TO ACCEPTING
THE CROSS

Pride goes before destruction, and a haughty spirit before a fall.
PROVERBS 16:18

The cross is such good news. So why doesn't everyone embrace it?

I'm convinced that the single biggest reason is our pride. Pride was the downfall of the devil and all his demons. So it is also the downfall of much of humankind.

After looking at the incredible, marvelous, amazing grace of God, we can only marvel that God would provide such rich forgiveness for undeserving worms as we are in our unregenerate state.

There are some professing Christians who edit our hymns and change lines like "Amazing grace, how sweet the sound that saved a wretch like me" to this: "Amazing grace, how sweet the sound that saved a *soul* like me." But such alterations and self-absorption with self-esteem are misguided. They don't recognize the reality of our sin.

The Bible says Jesus Christ came into the world to seek and to save that which is lost. Many ministers like to ask people the question, "Are you saved?" The problem is, so many people in this country assume they're saved because they've never believed they were lost. But one thing is absolutely sure: You cannot be saved unless you're lost.

The Bible tells us that "God resists the proud, but gives grace to the humble" (James 4:6). Humbling ourselves before God and acknowledging our sin and our lostness is what prepares us to receive His grace. We're wrong if we think, *I am a good person, I am righteous and holy and just, and I am going to accept God's grace.* No, His grace is for the wicked; God "justifies the *ungodly*" (Romans 4:5). This is a most astonishing thing, but we have to humble ourselves and say, "O Christ, I am that lost sinner, that ungodly one for whom You came and for whom You died."

Christ saves only the lost. Who needs a teacher? A person who is ignorant. Who needs a doctor? A person who is ill. Who needs a Savior? A person who is lost.

DID YOU KNOW?
Before Christianity, pride was considered a virtue, humility a weakness. It was the Judeo-Christian tradition that denounced pride and arrogance and elevated true humility.

You can have no dealings with the Savior unless you come to realize you're lost—realizing it in truth, knowing in your mind and your heart, that this is exactly what you are and that the wrath of Almighty God is what you deserve.

We have all been children of disobedience. As sinners in time past, "we *all* once conducted ourselves in the lusts of our flesh, fulfilling the desires of the flesh and of the mind, and were *by nature* children of wrath" (Ephesians 2:3).

But God "is rich in mercy" (Ephesians 2:4). How wonderful that is.

I always used to wonder, when I first became a Christian, why God would ever do what He did in giving His Son for us. Nobody else would do something like that.

Then I came across a text in Scripture that told me why. Why would God do that? Listen to this: "That in the ages to come He might show the exceeding riches of His grace in His kindness toward us in Christ Jesus" (Ephesians 2:7). Through the illimitable ages of eternity, God wants to show the exceeding riches of His grace in His kindness toward us. He wants us to know who and what He is. And when we begin to see this truth, we will learn as well who *we* really are—and what we are.

Note what the apostle Paul wrote about the message of the cross and how both unbelieving Jews and Gentiles rejected it because of their pride:

> For the message of the cross is foolishness to those who are perishing, but to us who are being saved it is the power of God. For it is written: "I will destroy the wisdom of the wise, and bring to nothing the understanding of the prudent." Where is the wise? Where is the scribe? Where is the disputer of this age? Has not God made foolish the wisdom of this world? For since, in the wisdom of God, the world through wisdom did not know God, it pleased God through the foolishness of the message preached to save those who believe. For Jews request a sign, and Greeks seek after wisdom; but we preach Christ crucified, to the Jews a stumbling block and to the Greeks foolishness, but to those who are called, both Jews and Greeks, Christ the power of God and the wisdom of God. Because the foolishness of God is wiser than men, and the weakness of God is stronger than men. (1 Corinthians 1:18–25)

The time has come to put away all our pride. Salvation is God's doing, not ours.

Prayer: Blessed Lord Jesus Christ,
You are the Savior of men and the hope
of the world. Teach us true humility so that
we may come to You with a childlike spirit.

"It was through Pride that
the devil became the devil."
(C. S. Lewis)

PART III
THE CROSS IN THE LAW
AND PROPHETS

9

THE CROSS IN THE OLD TESTAMENT

*Then I said to them, "If it is agreeable to you,
give me my wages; and if not, refrain."
So they weighed out for my wages thirty pieces of silver.*
ZECHARIAH 11:12

About a thousand years before Jesus came to earth, the prophets of Israel predicted the coming Messiah, an eternal king to rule the people. They predicted the cross—even before the grisly practice of crucifixion had been devised! Their prophecies were both specific and memorable. Christ clearly fulfilled the suffering servant strand of Old Testament prophecies.

Some people, when they hear the term *prophecies*, think about those unbelievable pseudo newspapers found at grocery store checkout counters, with screaming headlines about Hollywood stars and UFO sightings and alien invasions. But in the interplay of the Old and New Testaments, we find something that is truly incredible, yet verifiable. We find scores and scores of written statements, documented hundreds of years before Jesus Christ, that He fulfilled. Many of these statements point to His death and resurrection.

Indeed, Jesus fulfilled many prophecies of the Old Testament. As prophesied, He came from the line of Abraham (Genesis 12:3; Galatians 3:8), Isaac, and Jacob, and more specifically from the tribe of Judah (Genesis 49:10). Furthermore, He was from the house of David (Jeremiah 23:5) and was given the throne of David (Psalm 132:11). He was born of a virgin mother (Isaiah 7:14) in Bethlehem (Micah 5:2). And His throne has become an everlasting throne (Psalm 45:6). All these things were written about Him hundreds of years before He was born.

Stop and think, my friend. Suppose you were trying to describe the man who would be elected President of the United States in the year 2764. You prophesy that he will be born in a particular small town—let us say in Mississippi—a town so small it isn't even on most maps. You describe all of this person's lineage and things he will do and things that will happen to him during his lifetime. Also, you describe his cruel and unjust death.

"The prophecies foretold a twofold coming of Christ: the one, belonging already to history, was the coming of a dishonored and suffering man; the other shall take place when, as the prophets announced, he shall appear from heaven in glory with his angelic throng." (Justin Martyr)

The Old Testament describes how Jesus would be betrayed by a friend for a specific amount of money—thirty pieces of silver. (Can you likewise accurately say that this President in 2764 will be betrayed by a friend? And for how much money?)

There are two Old Testament passages in particular that take us to the foot of the cross—Psalm 22 and Isaiah 53. (They're so important that in this book we'll later devote a separate chapter to each of them.) Meanwhile, there are a multitude of other prophecies scattered throughout the Old Testament that deal with the cross or the events leading up to it.

Let's delve into a few of these, such as the prophecy that He would be forsaken by all His followers (Zechariah 13:7). This was written about 500 BC by the same prophet (Zechariah) who notes the amount of the betrayal price, and how it would be used to buy a potter's field (11:12–13). He also foretells this stunning cross-related prediction: "They will look on Me whom they pierced. Yes, they will mourn for Him as one mourns for his only son, and grieve for Him as one grieves for a firstborn" (Zechariah 12:10).

Writing about 250 years earlier (in c. 750 bc), the prophet Isaiah noted the Messiah would be scourged and spat upon (Isaiah 50:6).

Likewise we see in Scripture that He would be given gall and vinegar to drink (Psalm 69:21). He would be rejected as a cornerstone of the nation (Psalm 118:22). He would commend His spirit to God the Father (Psalm 31:5). Not a bone of His would be broken (Exodus 12:46). This last aspect is part of the theme of how Jesus is the Passover Lamb (we've dedicated a later chapter to that point as well).

The Old Testament says that the Messiah would become a high priest greater than Aaron—in the order of Melchizedek (Psalm 110:4). Old Testament priests offered animals before God, shedding blood to atone for sin, and all these sacrifices were shadows of the ultimate sacrifice of Jesus our High Priest, who offered Himself as a blood sacrifice to atone for sins.

After the cross, He would be raised from the dead (Psalm 16:10, written about 1000 BC). Then He would experience the triumphal effects of His cross and resurrection:

- He would ascend to heaven (Psalm 68:18).
- He would be seated at God's right hand (Psalm 110:1).

- He would become a smiting scepter (Psalm 2:9).
- He would rule the Gentiles (Psalm 2:8).

So we see that Christ fulfilled all sorts of prophecies in His life. But He also fulfilled many by His death. We'll focus on these in the next few chapters.

Prayer: Thank You, Lord, for fulfilling this host of prophecies, especially in Your suffering and death. Thank You for Your Word, which is trustworthy and true and which has no true rivals.

"The more I studied [the Old Testament prophecies fulfilled in Christ], the more difficulty I had in trying to explain them away." (former skeptic Lee Strobel)

THE FIRST PROMISE
OF THE GOSPEL

And I will put enmity between you and the woman,
and between your seed and her Seed; He shall bruise [crush]
your head and you shall bruise His heel.

<small>THE LORD GOD'S WORD TO THE SERPENT, IN GENESIS 3:15</small>

We've already noted how Jesus fulfilled a host of Old Testament prophecies. In the next few chapters, we want to examine a few of these in depth. Let's look especially at the very first promise of the cross we find in the Old Testament.

Early in the first book of the Bible, we find the first hint of the cross of Christ. Theologians call this promise of Genesis 3:15 the *Protovangelium*, the first gospel, that wondrous promise given by God to our first parents in Eden. The Garden of Eden was the only utopia man has ever known, that glorious paradise God created for them—where they had a marvelous relationship with their Creator, with one another, and with their environment.

Then disaster fell. The man and woman sinned and disobeyed God. Their skies turned black and their souls morose, and gloom hung over them like a pall. Sin had entered like venom into the veins of the human race, and with sin came death.

But in the midst of that stygian blackness, there appeared a single star—a star of prophetic hope, a star of promise. God said that the seed of the woman would destroy the head of the serpent, even though the serpent would wound the heel of the seed of the woman.

In all of Scripture there is no other person called the "seed of the woman." Everyone is begotten by man. In the chronologies of Christ we read how Abraham begat Isaac, who begat Jacob, who begat so and so, who begat David, who begat so and so, and so and so. Matthew lists one man after another, until we finally read "Jacob begot Joseph the husband of Mary, of whom [feminine pronoun] was born Jesus who is called Christ" (Matthew 1:16). And so, in the long history of the human race there is this single exception of Christ, the only one not begotten by man. He was the seed of the woman; His Father was God. That promise was given to our first parents and to their children and grandchildren, and it spread with them throughout the entire world.

And so, after man plunged into sin through Adam's rebellion, we found ourselves in a helpless state.

Thank God He didn't leave us there. Instead He gave us this promise, in Genesis 3:15, that the seed of the woman would destroy the head of the serpent. There would be the seed of the woman, Christ, who would come into the world and destroy the works of Satan. Christ accomplished this upon the cross.

DID YOU KNOW?
The whole Bible can be described in just three words:
Generation is what happens in Genesis 1 and 2. *Degeneration* is what happens in Genesis 3. And *Regeneration* is the story of all the rest of the Bible. That's why if we don't get Genesis 3 right, we will never understand the rest of Scripture.

Speaking to the serpent who tempted Adam and Eve to fall, God states in Genesis 3:15,

And I will put enmity
Between you and the woman,

And between your seed and her Seed;
He shall bruise [crush] your head
And you shall crush His heel.

When Christ was crucified, His heel was wounded, but in the process He crushed the head of the serpent.

In Mel Gibson's movie *The Passion of the Christ*, when Satan appears to tempt Jesus in the Garden of Gethsemane, he releases a snake that slithers toward Jesus while the Savior is prostrate on the ground in prayer. Christ then stands up and forcefully crushes the serpent's head with His heel. This is a symbolic acting out of this Scripture.

Back in the Garden of Eden, the man and woman had clothed themselves in fig leaf aprons of their own making. People have been doing much the same ever since, because one of the results of the Fall was, first of all, shame at our nakedness. Man retains the element of shame because of his sin, and he tries to cover himself up. In our case, we put on the fig leaves of our own self-righteousness, our own piety, morality, churchgoing, commandment-keeping, benevolence, or whatever it is. They're all fig leaves, and they won't really cover our shame and nakedness.

But then we read how God made a coat of skins and covered the man and woman with them—a foreshadowing of the great covering God would provide in His own Son. He is the Lamb of God, who would be slain and would rise again to clothe us with the white robes of His own perfect righteousness. Jesus was the only One who ever lived a perfect life. He was the Second Adam, and He succeeded where the first Adam failed.

Now we can be clothed with the white robes of the perfect righteousness of Jesus Christ and be cleansed by His blood, faultless to stand before the throne of God. We can be given a new nature. This new nature does, indeed, love God and love our neighbor and desires to do good to humanity. Only through the

power of the gospel and the regenerating power of the Holy
Spirit is there any hope for this nation and for this world. It is a
glorious hope, and it's a hope promised and foreshadowed for us
right here in the third chapter of Genesis. It is a magnificent,
marvelous story.

---

*Prayer: Heavenly Father, thank You for
sending Your Son, who crushed the head of
the serpent even though His own heel and
hands and side were pierced. Amen.*

In Adam's Fall,
We sinned all....
Christ crucify'd,
For sinners dy'd.
(*New England Primer*)

11

THE CROSS
IN PSALM 22

They pierced My hands and My feet.
PSALM 22:16

D id you know that a thousand years before Jesus was crucified, we find an uncanny description that essentially
takes us to the foot of the cross?

In Psalm 22, David describes his own sufferings—and in so
doing, he foretells the greater event to come some ten centuries
later.

David had come to the throne of Israel in 1010 BC Because
of the prophecies in Psalm 22, which were later fulfilled, his
words provide a clear example of the inspiration of the Scriptures.
Only an inspired Word would be able to prophesy all the things
contained herein.

Dr. Charles Augustus Briggs has said that you can take this
psalm and lay it side by side with the New Testament accounts
of the crucifixion of Christ and see how they dovetail perfectly.
It is astonishing that someone could describe something so intimately and intricately a thousand years before it happened.

The psalm opens with this line: "My God, My God, why
have You forsaken Me?" Immediately we're plunged into the
depths of Christ's anguish on the cross, the agony of His crucifixion, and those hours of darkness. Christ has, as it were,
descended into the very blackness of hell, and God has poured
out His wrath upon Him after man has done his worst.

The psalm's opening continues:

Why are You so far from helping Me,
And from the words of My groaning?

This is a unique cry. Maybe you never realized this before, but Jesus rarely refers to God as "My God." He almost always refers to Him as "My Father." But not here.

What would it mean to endure hell? What would it be like to endure hell for a world of sinners? Jesus was finding out. *This* is what caused Him, the night before, to extrude blood through His pores—the absolute, unbelievable agony of enduring the wrath of God. So mind-boggling, so staggering, so vast is His pain that God seems to have forsaken Him. And...*He has.*

DID YOU KNOW?
When Psalm 22 was written in 1000 BC, crucifixion was not yet in use as a form of execution. It was developed by the Phoenicians about four centuries later, then picked up much later by the Romans. And yet, many centuries before all of that, David, by the Spirit of prophecy, writes, "They pierced My hands and My feet."

I've heard liberal preachers say, "Jesus just *thought* God forsook Him; but, of course, He didn't." Wrong. His being forsaken by God is what the cross is all about. Jesus was God-forsaken in order that *we* might not be. In such blinding, numbing agony, His human nature cries out, "Why have You forsaken Me?" Everyone had forsaken Him, but most importantly, God the Father had forsaken Him.

David's psalm also includes these prophetic lines:

I am poured out like water,
And all My bones are out of joint;

My heart is like wax;
It has melted within Me.
My strength is dried up like a potsherd,
And My tongue clings to My jaws. (22:14–15)

And so, we see all of Christ's bones out of joint—an indication of the agonies of crucifixion, which tended to pull the bones out of joint in the body as a person hung upon a cross. And we see an intimation of His cry, "I thirst," when David speaks of his tongue clinging to his jaws and his strength being "dried up."

David continues:

For dogs have surrounded Me;
The congregation of the wicked has enclosed Me.
 (22:16)

This indicates that He was stationary, while others were around Him.

Then we see the terrible means of Christ being affixed to the cross:

They pierced My hands and My feet. (22:16)

David continues:

I can count all My bones.
They look and stare at Me. (22:16–17)

The soldiers had stripped Christ naked, and with His bones all being pulled out of joint, there He hangs on the cross in this shameful position of nakedness and horror and agony before the crowd, many of whom were just standing there watching this horrible spectacle.

We see the prophecy of what the soldiers did with His robe while Jesus hung naked on the cross:

They divide My garments among them,
And for My clothing they cast lots. (22:18)

Then there comes the most amazing prophecy fulfilled at the cross:

All the ends of the world
Shall remember and turn to the LORD,
And all the families of the nations
Shall worship before You.
For the kingdom is the LORD's,
And He rules over the nations. (22:27–28)

When hundreds of millions of Christians attend church worldwide each week, we help fulfill this very prophecy of all the ends of the world remembering His death on our behalf. The gospel of Jesus Christ is being spread into every nation—even in places where it's highly illegal.

What an incredible psalm this is.

---

*Prayer: Thank You, Jesus, that what David
saw from a distance, we can see close up—
You, pierced for our transgressions.*

"It would be mathematically impossible for anyone else ever to fulfill all these parameters of prophecy in the Old Testament any better than Jesus did."
(Paul L. Maier)

12

THE CROSS
IN ISAIAH 53

All we like sheep have gone astray;
we have turned, every one, to his own way;
and the LORD has laid on Him the iniquity of us all.

ISAIAH 53:6

While King David, in Psalm 22, takes us to the foot of the cross, the Hebrew prophet Isaiah explains its meaning to us. Jesus did not just die an agonizing death—He accomplished something meaningful through it.

One of the most remarkable passages of the Old Testament, which speaks so clearly about Jesus Christ, is Isaiah 53. I think it's interesting that this passage of Isaiah 53 is virtually never read in the synagogue today. Why? Because it so evidently points to Jesus Christ that it's an embarrassment for them to read it.

I hope you'll read it now, familiarize yourself with it, and perhaps even take time to memorize it.

Here is most of that chapter (consider that these lines were written about 700 BC):

> ³ He is despised and rejected by men,
> A Man of sorrows and acquainted with grief.
> And we hid, as it were, our faces from Him;
> He was despised, and we did not esteem Him.
> ⁴ Surely He has borne our griefs
> And carried our sorrows;

Yet we esteemed Him stricken,
Smitten by God, and afflicted.
⁵ But He was wounded for our transgressions,
He was bruised for our iniquities;
The chastisement for our peace was upon Him,
And by His stripes we are healed.
⁶ All we like sheep have gone astray;
We have turned, every one, to his own way;
And the LORD has laid on Him the iniquity of us all.
⁷ He was oppressed and He was afflicted,
Yet He opened not His mouth;
He was led as a lamb to the slaughter,
And as a sheep before its shearers is silent,
So He opened not His mouth.
⁸ He was taken from prison and from judgment,
And who will declare His generation?
For He was cut off from the land of the living;
For the transgressions of My people He was stricken.
⁹ And they made His grave with the wicked—
But with the rich at His death,
Because He had done no violence,
Nor was any deceit in His mouth.
¹⁰ Yet it pleased the LORD to bruise Him;
He has put Him to grief.
When You make His soul an offering for sin,
He shall see His seed, He shall prolong His days,
And the pleasure of the LORD shall prosper in His hand.
¹¹ He shall see the labor of His soul, and be satisfied.
By His knowledge My righteous Servant shall justify
many,
For He shall bear their iniquities.
¹² Therefore I will divide Him a portion with the great,
And He shall divide the spoil with the strong,

Because He poured out His soul unto death,
And He was numbered with the transgressors,
And He bore the sin of many,
And made intercession for the transgressors.

Picture sheep gamboling along over the hills, stupidly falling over cliffs, getting themselves entangled, falling into rivers and drowning. That's what we're like, according to verse 6 in this chapter. We have turned to our own way. "I did it my way," says the song, and that sentiment is repeated by many who ultimately drive their life into a ditch—if not in this world, then in that eternal ditch.

Christ was the One who was oppressed and afflicted for us: "For the transgressions of My people He was stricken" (53:8).

We know that He was crucified between two thieves, and in the grave of Joseph of Arimathea, a rich man, He was buried. So the prophecy was fulfilled in every detail: "And they made His grave with the wicked—but with the rich at His death" (53:9).

We read here also that "it pleased the LORD to bruise Him"

> Isaiah 53 is a picture of an individual—a suffering Messiah—who came to die for us. The opposing idea—that this passage refers instead to the state of Israel—first appeared about AD 1100. Later in that same century, the greatest medieval authority of Jewish tradition and law—Maimonides—said that this interpretation was a false use of this prophecy. This great Jewish scholar and authority was saying that Isaiah 53 did refer to an individual Messiah—the same view that had prevailed among Jews throughout prior centuries.

(53:10). Why did this death please Him? Not because it was pleasant, but because "God so loved the world that He gave His only begotten Son" (John 3:16), who gave His life a ransom for many.

The Jews in the Old Testament knew the Messiah would be

a great high priest to offer sacrifices, but they never dreamt He would offer *Himself* as a sacrifice.

Today, when confronted with this prophecy from the Old Testament, a Jewish person is most likely to say that this suffering Savior, this righteous one described in Isaiah 53, refers to the state of Israel. My friend, that just won't wash—not even according to great Jewish scholars. Any investigation of this makes it clear that this will not do.

Why did He come? Isaiah tells us why: He came to bear our sorrows; He came to be struck down by God and to be afflicted on our behalf.

Prayer: Dear Lord, we confess that we like sheep have gone our own way, but we thank You that You didn't leave us. Instead, You sent the Good Shepherd and let Him bear our iniquity, in our place.

"In Isaiah chapter 53 we have almost a running commentary on what happened on Good Friday to Jesus." (Paul L. Maier)

13

JESUS OUR JOSHUA

*"And she will bring forth a Son, and you shall call
His name JESUS, for He will save His people from their sins."*
THE ANGEL OF THE LORD TO JOSEPH, IN MATTHEW 1:21

Before Jesus was born, the angel of God who announced His birth announced His name too: Jesus. But why the name *Jesus*?

Jesus is an English word, derived from the Greek word *Iesous*. The name He grew up in Nazareth with was Joshua, or Jehoshua, as it would sound in Hebrew. And of course Joshua was the name of a great hero of the Old Testament, the captain who led the people of God into the Promised Land.

Here is brought out a great truth that everybody needs to understand: "For the law was given through Moses, but grace and truth came through Jesus Christ" (John 1:17).

The whole message of the Bible, as Martin Luther liked to say, is divided into two parts: law and grace, or law and gospel—these two things. But most people have never gotten past the first half.

Consequently, they're basing their religion, their salvation, their hope of heaven upon the law—upon keeping some set of precepts. Whether it be the Old Testament, the Ten Commandments, the Golden Rule, the Sermon on the Mount, or whatever, they believe that by following some set of rules, they will one day enter the Promised Land.

But the whole message of the Bible is personified in the persons of Moses and Joshua. Moses represents the law in that he was the agent through whom God gave the law to the world. Joshua represents Jesus, who brought us grace and truth.

If you're basing your hope of entering the Promised Land on Moses and the law, reflect upon the fact that Moses himself never made it. He died in the wilderness, having seen the Promised Land from afar. Thus God is telling us that the law is inadequate to bring us into that promised home—to that land on high.

DID YOU KNOW?
"Jehovah saves" or "Jehovah is salvation"—that is what the name Joshua (Jesus) means. Through the cross, Jehovah saves.

Jesus, on the other hand, has gone ahead and prepared for us a place in heaven, just as Joshua in the Old Testament was the one who brought the people of Israel into the Promised Land. He was the one who fought against the Canaanites, Hittites, Philistines, and all the others who infested that land. He made it possible for the Hebrew people to move into those ordained lots that God had provided for the twelve tribes of Israel. But *our* Joshua—Jesus—is far greater than the Old Testament Joshua. In fact, there are many contrasts between these two.

For example, Joshua of old led a vast army—a great force, a multitude—against the hosts of the adversaries. But our greater-than-Joshua, our Jesus, fought the battles alone, against all of God's foes and ours. He fought the battle of temptation in the wilderness alone. He fought the battle against Satan alone. He fought the battle in the Garden of Gethsemane alone, when that horrid cup containing all the sin of the world and its distillation was set before His face. When He saw all of our iniquity and all of our vile foulness, Christ faced that alone. Though He perspired, as it were, great drops of blood, He nevertheless took that cup to His lips and drank it down. Jesus Christ, the pure and holy One who never sinned, became Sin. He trod the winepress alone.

There in the darkness of Calvary, at midday, the wrath of God was poured out upon Him alone. When all the demons of hell, like lions roaring out of the pit, came to sink their claws and fangs in Him, He fought them all alone. There were no angelic hosts, though He could have called upon them in an instant. There was no great army behind Him. Even His faithful friends had fled Him. Even His Father forsook Him. Jesus was alone.

Therefore, we should never forget that our salvation is through Jesus *alone*. Not Jesus plus anything else. Not Jesus plus you. Not Jesus plus the church. Not Jesus plus anything.

Christ saves us totally. "He will save His people from their sins"—that's what His name means (Matthew 1:21).

Prayer: Thank You, Jesus our Joshua, that while Moses reminds us of our failings—and they are many— You fought the powers of hell in order to bring us home one day to the true Promised Land.

"[Moses] remained on the hill until evening with his arms stretched out and supported, representing the type (foreshadowing) of the cross; the other, whose byname was Jesus, took charge of the battle and led Israel to victory." (Justin Martyr)

14

CHRIST OUR PASSOVER

So this day shall be to you a memorial; and you shall keep
it as a feast to the LORD throughout your generations.
You shall keep it as a feast by an everlasting ordinance.

EXODUS 12:14

In the hardness of his heart, Pharaoh had defied the Almighty God. And so God sent plague after plague onto the land of Egypt with ever-increasing severity, including these:

- The blood that crimsoned the Nile and their pools and wells and fountains.
- The locusts that swarmed their fields, consuming everything.
- The black darkness—so dark it was practically palpable.

But in all these things Pharaoh hardened his heart, until Jehovah declared one last plague:

"About midnight I will go out into the midst of Egypt; and all the firstborn in the land of Egypt shall die, from the firstborn of Pharaoh who sits on his throne, even to the firstborn of the female servant who is behind the handmill, and all the firstborn of the animals." (Exodus 11:4–5)

So Moses gathered the people of God together and told them what God had said. They were instructed to take a lamb from out of their flocks on the tenth day of what was to become the first month of the year for them, the month of *Abib*. They were to keep this lamb until the fourteenth day of the same month. Then they were to slay it—a lamb without spot and blemish, a lamb of the first year. They were not to boil it in water but were to roast and eat it, along with unleavened bread and bitter herbs. They were to eat what would later become known as the Passover meal.

But first they were to take candles and search carefully into every cabinet, into every closet, into every nook and cranny of their houses to see if they could find any leaven—a perfect picture of sin, the corruption that spreads throughout the body and that destroys the human life, as sin always does. If any was found, they were to burn it in fire so that they might worthily partake of this meal.

Centuries later, Paul would declare, "Get rid of the old yeast that you may be a new batch without yeast—as you really are. For Christ, our Passover lamb, has been sacrificed" (1 Corinthians 5:7, NIV).

DID YOU KNOW?
When Christ instituted the Last Supper, He was participating in the Passover with His disciples, thus both fulfilling and continuing the ancient custom.

Most crucially of all, the Hebrews were to take a bunch of hyssop, dip it in the blood in the basin, and strike the top and two sides of the doorposts of their houses—forming a rudimentary sign of the cross. They were not to go out the door of their houses until the morning, because at midnight the Lord would send His angel to destroy the firstborn throughout all Egypt. But whenever the angel of death would see the blood upon the doorpost and the lintels, he would pass over those homes.

When that fatal night came, all Egypt was asleep. Beside, the mighty pyramid of Cheops, the Sphinx—that stone amalgam of beast and man—looked out with inscrutable gaze over the white moonlit desert. A thousand villages up and down the Nile were quietly asleep. And in his marble palace, flanked by porphyry columns, Egypt's great Pharaoh slumbered in his bed. Around those columns were entwined sculptured serpents crowned with harsh-looking eagles whose eyes flashed with precious jewels.

All Egypt slumbered.

Finally, in the darkest time of the night—at the midnight hour—a shriek was heard…then another…and another. All over Egypt there rose up a cry of alarm…a lament and a wail…moaning and crying. This was a sorrow unlike any that had ever been heard before, nor would ever be heard again.

Meanwhile, inside the houses of the Hebrews, the people waited, dreading to hear the wave of mourning approaching their own houses. But seeing the blood upon the doorposts and lintels, God's angel of death passed over them.

The Passover celebration continued down through the centuries, and when Christ our Savior came, John the Baptist pointed Him out at the beginning of His ministry with these words: "Behold! The Lamb of God, who takes away the sin of the world!" (John 1:29). Not the lamb of a household or of a nation and not the sins of an individual or a family. But the Lamb *of God*, who takes away the sin *of all the world* for all time—for all those who will trust in Him.

So Christ was the true Passover Lamb that the lambs of old merely pointed toward. He was the One who alone could truly take away sin and bring forgiveness. He was not called the Passover Lamb because such a sacrifice existed before; rather, that sacrifice was instituted because God had determined beforehand that He would send a true sacrifice for sins—the One in whom we must hide if we would be spared from the wrath of God.

We need to remember that apart from His protective blood shed on the cross, we have no hope. In providing that blood, it was necessary that the Lamb should die.

Substitution. Propitiation. The innocent dying for the guilty. This was God's omnipotent plan—that pure innocence should die for utter depravity. So Christ came to be the Lamb who takes away the sin of the world.

Prayer: O Lord Jesus Christ, the true Passover Lamb of God, come and cleanse me and empower me by Your Spirit that I may live henceforth a holy life.

"Christ is spoken of as a lamb because [of] his willingness and his goodness, by which he made God again propitious to men and bestowed pardon for sins." (Origen)

15

THE NEW COVENANT

Behold, the days are coming,
says the LORD, when I will make a new covenant
with the house of Israel and with the house of Judah.
JEREMIAH 31:31

According to the Bible, every person who ever has been or ever will be saved is saved by grace.

God placed Adam and Eve, our forefathers, under a covenant—a covenant of works. Now a covenant involves at least two parties, the greater and the lesser. It also involves a condition, and it also involves promises.

For Adam and Eve, the condition was very simple: They were to simply obey one command from God—to not eat the fruit from the tree of the knowledge of good and evil.

And yet Adam, who was the federal head of the human race, sinned and plunged both himself and all his posterity into guilt and corruption and death. And that, of course, was a great tragedy.

In response, God could have simply let the various aspects of the covenant of works work their way out: All of Adam's descendants would be born with a sinful nature, they would grow up and express this sinful nature in all the different kinds of iniquity, they would die, and then finally they would be judged and condemned to hell. This would happen generation after generation. That's all God needed to let happen, for it would be perfect justice (God *must* be just; He doesn't have to be merciful). That would be the history of the world.

But God had another plan—a plan that had begun long before the creation of the universe. In the distant councils of the Trinity in eternity past, God foresaw that Adam would fail, and He laid forth His plan. He would be gracious, and He would extend to man *another* covenant—this time a covenant of grace. For it was obvious that if under the most perfect conditions man could not pass a covenant of works, his only hope was pure unmerited grace.

> DID YOU KNOW?
> If Adam and Eve had merely kept that one command—just that one—they would have gained eternal life for themselves and all posterity, and we would never have known sin. There would be no war. There would be no crime. There would be no vileness and corruption in the world. This world would be a paradise. It took the sacrifice of Christ on the cross to regain all that for us.

God the Father looked down through the ages to come and He saw a sinful world as a result of Adam's sin. He decided He would choose—out of the vast multitude of sinful, rebellious, ungodly, and unbelieving people—a host of people who would be His seed, His chosen ones, His elect.

And to take care of the problem of their sin, He decided He would send His Son to earth. And so His Son, the eternal Word of God (later to become the Christ), agreed that He would come into this world, where He would take upon Himself a human body. He came to live as the Second Adam. Thus, He would perfectly obey all God's commandments and thus fulfill the covenant of works in our place that Adam failed to fulfill. He endured the wrath of God and of men, finally being scourged, condemned, and crucified for us.

The Holy Spirit was the enabler of all this. He provided the inspiration for the Scriptures that would explain it. He created the body for Christ in the womb of Mary. He is the One who regenerates the seed and creates this people of God called Christians. He is the One who sanctifies them and preserves them until that great day when they shall come to see Christ face-to-face.

Do you remember reading in Genesis 15 where Abraham's sacrifices were cut in half and laid on either side? And so we find God moving through these sacrifices and pronouncing an oath. It was a malediction, a curse upon Himself if He should ever violate this oath. Since God could not swear by any one greater (because there is none), He swore by Himself that should He ever violate this covenant, He Himself would be divided in half, even as these sacrifices were, and the immutable, unchangeable God would be changed. Therefore Abraham could know that this was true, because God had sworn it Himself.

In the Old Covenant, the rites God initiated with His people were all bloody—the blood of circumcision, the blood of the Passover lamb, the blood of all the different sacrificial animals. All of those foreshadowed the coming of the Son of God, for the Old Testament sacrifices couldn't really take away sin.

Now Christ comes, the eternal Son, and on the cross He sheds His blood—and *that* was the end of the shedding of blood. There and then, at three o'clock on Good Friday, came the final sacrifice, the end of the shedding of blood. And so the bloody rite of circumcision gives way to the rite of baptism in the new covenant. The bloody rite of the Passover gives way to the Lord's Supper. And all the sacrificial animals slain by the thousands disappear, for the blood of Christ pays for the sins of all those who ever are saved.

Prayer: Father, we stand in awe and
amazed at Your love. Thank You, O God,
for providing our sacrifice through Your Son.

"Grace is but glory begun, and glory is
but grace perfected." (Jonathan Edwards)

16

EDEN REVISITED

The LORD God planted a garden eastward in Eden,
and there He put the man whom He had formed.

GENESIS 2:8

B ecause of the cross, we have Eden revisited.

Man is nearer to God in a garden than anywhere else on earth, or so the couplet goes. I'm afraid for many people today, that's merely a poor excuse for not attending church. But there's certainly an element of truth in it, something we might call a genetic homesickness, because man began his sojourn on this earth in a garden—a garden in Eden. As a matter of fact, we're told that man will conclude his sojourn in a garden.

Jesus said to the penitent thief on the cross, "Today you will be with Me in Paradise" (Luke 23:43). The Persian word *paradeiso* means "a beautiful and enclosed garden." Within the city of God, we're told that in the future there will be a crystal river flowing forth from the throne of God, and the Tree of Life will be there with twelve kinds of fruit for the healing of the nations.

There's something wonderful about a garden. And in the second chapter of Genesis, we go back to Eden, our ancestral home, to discover some of the things God has done for man and what He intended for us to do here on this earth.

The word *Eden* comes from a word meaning "delight." It's a garden of delight. And so it was. In it God planted every tree that was pleasant to the eye and good for food. Everything needed was provided, and it was beautiful.

We're told that God planted the garden in Eden. By the way, Eden was not just a garden; Eden was the whole area—just as in the City of God, there will be a garden.

I've seen some marvelous gardens. The most impressive were at Versailles, outside Paris. The incredible palace of Versailles is absolutely gigantic. It took practically all the wealth of France to build this palace, and it is mind-boggling in its enormity, huge beyond imagining. I think it would take a week to see all its rooms. For a year after seeing it, my mind on occasion would return to it in astonishment. And behind it, magnificent gardens stretch as far as the eye can see.

But all this is nothing compared to the Garden of Eden, because *God* planted that one. All other gardens are merely the creations of men, while God made and

"...the second Adam, Christ, steps into the breach: in death and resurrection he breaks the power of death and brings new life..." (Eberhard Arnold)

planted the garden in Eden. How glorious it must have been, for God is the ultimate artist. He had created the cosmos out of chaos. What does *cosmos* mean? It comes from the same word as *cosmetics*; it's a thing of beauty.

Because of the sin of the first Adam, society sinks deeper into the mire of sin and guilt. But thank God, there's another Adam— a Second Adam—God's Son. God provided a bride for that first Adam—Eve was created from a rib that God took out of Adam's side while he was in a deep sleep.

Likewise God also has provided a bride for the second Adam. *We* are that bride. And in order to get this bride, Christ's side also was pierced—it was pierced as He hung there upon the cross at Golgotha. But there was no deep sleep for Him. There was no anesthesia. Even a mild form of vinegar and gall was refused by Christ, that He might experience the pain that sin properly deserves. This pain is something that *we* must endure forever if He does not endure it for us.

And so, in body and soul, Jesus endured an infinite penalty that we might be spared, that His bride might be brought into existence. He did this so that we might leave our earthly background and parents and cleave to Him as our bridegroom. Thus a whole new family—the family of God—would be created.

I trust that you're part of this bride created by the piercing of Christ's side. I hope you've turned your back upon this worldly system, with its lust and pride of life, and are cleaving to Christ as Savior and Lord. That's what faith is—holding to Him as your only hope in this life and in the world to come. It means resting upon, clinging to, cleaving to the living Christ.

This is the way in which our Bridegroom, our Savior, will take us into the paradise on high, the new garden of Eden, and the blessed perfection He has prepared for us.

Prayer: Help us to cling to You, O God,
and to look unto Him whose side was pierced
that the bride might come forth. Join us to Him
that we might cleave to Him forever.

"Every woman who plants marigolds by her front steps displays her longing for Eden." (Kirsti S. Newcombe)

17

BORN TO DIE

...the Lamb slain from the foundation of the world.

REVELATION 13:8

Have you ever asked children what they want to be when they get older? "Tell me, Sarah, what do you want to be when you grow up?"

"Oh, I'm going to be an astronaut."

"And how about you, Blake?"

"I'm going to be the President of the United States."

"And how about you, Jason?"

"I'm going to be a major league baseball player."

And how about you, Jesus? What do You plan to be when You grow up?

This would be His answer: "Dead. Dead. That's what I plan to be when I grow up. Because, you see, that's why I was born. I was born to die."

Everyone was born for something—to be a doctor, lawyer, teacher, minister...a thousand other things. But Jesus was born for the specific purpose of dying. Unlike every other child who has ever been born, who was born to live, Jesus Christ was born to die.

That was a decision made long ago in eternity. Revelation tells us He was the Lamb slain before the foundation of the earth. Before God ever created the Milky Way or the Andromeda galaxy or spun the nebulae out into space, Jesus Christ was slain in the mind of God. He was crucified before the foundation of the world. He came to die in order that we might not have to. He came to die because we deserve to die. He came to pay the penalty He alone could pay.

His was the most amazing birth in all of history, because it was not merely a birth. This was an incarnation, as the ever-living God became incarnate in human flesh—God Incarnate. The word *incarnate* isn't common in the vocabulary of most Americans today. But they probably would recognize chili con carne, which means, of course, chili beans *con* ("with") *carne* ("flesh"). So God Incarnate means God in human flesh. The great foundational belief of the Christian religion all over the world is that two thousand years ago, the almighty and eternal God came and walked among us as a human being. This little planet was visited by the great God Almighty—in full demonstration of His love.

"How much do you love me?" a father once asked his five-year-old, sitting on his knee.

The little boy extended his arms and said, "That much, Daddy."

"Is that all?" the father asked.

The little boy stretched his arms even further, straining to do so. "No, Daddy, this much!"

The world had wondered about God for centuries, wanting to know if He really did love them, and if so, how much. Jesus came, and on a cross He answered that question when He died—with arms extended.

I was talking to a man one time, and he told me he didn't go
to church anymore, and I asked him why. He gave me the usual
stereotypical answers: "Well you see, that's my only day to sleep in,
and I've got other things I have to do." He added two
or three other reasons.

Roman citizens were not to be crucified. Cicero declared,
"Let the very name of the cross be far away from Roman
citizens; not from their bodies only, but from their thoughts,
their eyes, and their ears."

Much to his surprise, I told him, "Those aren't the reasons
you don't go to church." He looked at me in amazement, and I
continued: "I know the reason why you don't go to church. You
see, I've been on both sides of this equation. I didn't go for ten
years, but now I do. The reason you don't go to church is that
you've never personally experienced the love of Jesus Christ.
That's why you don't go."

Another man was at our church for a Christmas Eve
Communion service, where I was preaching about the love of
Christ. He said that as I explained Christ's love, he felt something
happening in his body, and he didn't know what it was. "I know
now," he told me, "that it was my hard, cold heart melting within
me. And by the time the service was over, I knew I had been
changed." He became a faithful Christian thereafter.

I know from personal experience that when I first encoun-
tered the love of Jesus Christ, my life was changed. I've often said
the love of Christ is like a screwdriver that God placed in my
"want-er," and He simply turned it upside down. Before that
time, I didn't go to church because I didn't *want* to; I didn't read
the Bible because I didn't *want* to. But now my want-er was
changed: I wanted to go to church, I wanted to learn about Christ
in the Bible, and I wanted to share Him with other people.

I had been changed by the love of Jesus Christ, who was born to die on the cross. And that kind of change, my friend, is the greatest thing you'll ever know in this world.

Prayer: Dearest Savior, Your death has given us life. Your wounds have made us whole. May we die to ourselves and live for You.

"The love of God is no mere sentimental feeling; it is redemptive power."
(Charles Clayton Morrison)

❧

18

CUR DEUS HOMO?

And the Word became flesh and dwelt among us.

JOHN 1:14

H ave you ever heard of the Latin phrase *cur Deus homo?*
Deus, as you know, means God, while *homo*, of course,
refers to man. But *cur*? Dog? No, that word means "why."
Therefore, we have "Why God man?" which happens to be the
title of one of the greatest of the Christian classics, written 900
years ago by Anselm, the Archbishop of Canterbury. He explored
this question: Why did God become man?

Indeed, why *did* God become man? Why was it necessary for
the infinitely glorious, omnipotent Creator of all the universe,
who fashioned the galaxies, to step out of His ivory palace into
the filth of a stable and become man?

"If we could but see God, we would know how we ought to
live." So said Socrates. The Greeks worshiped truth, goodness,
and beauty, and they thought that if anyone could only see perfect truth and perfect goodness and perfect beauty, such a person
would immediately know how he ought to live his life. He would
gladly follow in that path.

One day Truth descended from heaven and became incarnate in Jesus of Nazareth, who is the Way, the Truth, and the
Life. He is truth incarnate—and goodness incarnate as well, for
in Him there was found no sin. He is the altogether lovely One,
the Rose of Sharon, the Lily of the Valley, the Delightful One,
and the Perfect One in whom all is in perfect symmetry. Every

quality of human virtue was in perfect balance in Him.

He came and walked among us, and when we saw Him...*we hated Him*! With rough hands we took Him and threw Him on the ground and nailed Him to a cross because He was a mirror showing us our wrinkles and our warts and our ugliness and our sin. We nailed Him to a tree; then we buried Him in the ground out of sight and mind.

Amazing love,
How can it be,
That Thou my God
Shouldst die for me?
(Charles Wesley)

So we saw God in His perfection, as Socrates longed for mankind to see, but we didn't respond the way he thought we would. Socrates knew little or nothing about the true depths of the depravity of the human heart. No, our condition requires something far greater than seeing a perfect exemplar like Christ. Being our example is not the ultimate reason *cur Deus homo*.

You hear people say, "Oh, Jesus was a great teacher. That's why He came—to teach us." There's no doubt He was a great teacher; He was the greatest Teacher who ever taught, the paragon of pedagogic expertise.

I think of one skeptic who set about to write a book in which he was going to debunk Christ and get rid of the idea of His deity. As he began to do his research and to read about this One, he was astonished right from the very beginning. He read about this man

...who was born in a stable;

...who lived in a country bumpkin town (it was a byword: "Can anything good come out of Nazareth?" John 1:46);

...who never went to school ("How does this Man know letters, having never studied?" John 7:15);

...who never went to college or university;

...who never had a degree;

...who never traveled broadly;

and who then emerged out of total obscurity, walked up on

a mountain, and delivered the most monumental discourse on human ethics the world had ever heard.

The skeptic was stunned. How could this be? Indeed, he was so stunned that the hardened veneer of his unbelief began to crack, and soon he bowed the knee before Christ.

Yes, Christ was the greatest teacher who ever lived. Let me sum up His teaching for you, bring it all down to the bottom line, and in one sentence tell you the very essence of what Jesus taught. Surely you will want to know what is the essence of the teaching of the greatest Teacher who ever lived, correct?

Here it is—the culmination of the teaching of Jesus Christ: "Therefore you shall be perfect, just as your Father in heaven is perfect" (Matthew 5:48). With those words He stripped us bare of all our subterfuges and left us naked before God in all our iniquity.

In short, we don't have an excuse anymore, now that we know. The teaching of Jesus Christ condemns us one and all.

But God became a man to pay the infinite price for us. Only He could pay the price. If He were merely a man, He would not be the divine Savior. We would still be in our sins.

Prayer: Thank You, Lord Jesus, for leaving
Your throne above and emptying Yourself of all but
love and dying for Adam's helpless race.

"Man hath sinned, but
God hath suffered."
(Richard Hooker)

19

THE INCARNATION OF LOVE

Let this mind be in you which was also in Christ Jesus, who, being in the form of God, did not consider it robbery to be equal with God, but made Himself of no reputation, taking the form of a bondservant, and coming in the likeness of men. And being found in appearance as a man, He humbled Himself and became obedient to the point of death, even the death of the cross.

PHILIPPIANS 2:5–8

One Christmas, radio preacher Steve Brown asked his listeners if they'd ever stopped to think how the manger in Bethlehem was "really a big hug from God—who you thought was just a policeman!"

God is not a policeman. He's not an old man with a gray beard keeping track of all your individual sins. He is the great God of love who thus loved the world enough to give His own and only and eternal Son for us.

Jesus left the ivory palace of heaven in order to experience hell for us. His becoming a man is really the incarnation of love. He was God incarnate, and John tells us that God is love (he says this twice in the fourth chapter of the first letter of John, verses 8 and 16: "God is love"). So Jesus is really love incarnate as well—the incarnation, or fleshing out, of love.

In school we learned the three R's—"readin', 'ritin', and 'rithmetic." Well, there are also three R's of the incarnation—of why Christ came.

The first is *reconciliation*. Jesus came as the incarnate Deity to reconcile us unto God. The requirements to live at God's address in paradise are very simple: sinlessness and perfection. There can be no sin, so perfect obedience to all God's command- ments is required. (Those are exactly the criteria the angels possess.)

The incarnation is what frees us from hopelessness. As Augustine wrote, "We could despair of ourselves, unless he had been 'made flesh and dwelt amongst us.'" The incarnation is a reminder that God made Himself known to humanity— and though He may remain hidden to some, this is only because they are not looking to Christ.

I am happy to announce that I have those requirements — no sin and perfect obedience. I would hasten to add that though I own them, I didn't earn them; though I have them, I didn't live them. Jesus Christ was the sinless One. He was the One that perfectly obeyed God. He was the One who could say, "I always do those things that please Him [My Father]" (John 8:29). Which one of us could say that? And that perfect life Christ lived is given to me and to all those who will trust in Him by faith. It's given to us as a white robe. Clothed with the robe of Christ's righteousness, we may stand faultless in the presence of God.

The second R is *resurrection*. In the familiar carol "Hark! The Herald Angels Sing," the hymnist Charles Wesley said that Jesus was "born that man no more may die." What a glorious thing that is. Christ is the greatest person who ever lived because He meets our greatest need—the need to overcome death, which hangs like a black cloud over the world. It hangs over the horizon of every life. It gets closer and closer and larger and darker with every passing year. Yet Jesus Christ ban- ishes that cloud. He "has abolished death and brought life and immortality to light through the gospel" (2 Timothy 1:10).

On that first Easter morning, Christ the great Conqueror went forth to battle with the powers of darkness. There at Calvary, Jesus Christ took upon Himself all of the forces of hell. They fell upon Him, and in that struggle Christ appeared vanquished. His head fell upon His chest and He "yielded up His spirit" (Matthew 27:50). He ceased to breathe. A dark pall sank over all of the land. The hope of mankind was dashed, for His followers had thought He would be the Messiah and Savior of Israel.

Three days later, as the sun began to break over the eastern hills, out of that tomb, from out of the darkness of death, from out of the very pit of hell, there stepped forth One who could say, "I am He who lives, and was dead, and behold, I am alive forevermore" (Revelation 1:18). The word that had originally said "Jesus defeated" now went out again: "Jesus defeated death!" It was sounded first as a whisper...then a cry...then a shout...a chime sublime. Jesus defeated death, and He has brought life and immortality to light. He came to bring us not only reconciliation with God, but also an everlasting resurrection to paradise.

The third R is that He came to bring *regeneration*. Again in "Hark! The Herald Angels Sing," we sing that Jesus was "born to raise the sons of earth; born to give them second birth." The new birth is a mystery that has puzzled the minds of countless millions of people ever since that night when Nicodemus came to Jesus and was told, "Most assuredly, I say to you, unless one is born again, he cannot see the kingdom of God" (John 3:3).

There is a second birth, a spiritual birth that comes when we place our trust in Christ, when we invite Him to come into our heart and change our lives. The Bible also talks about a second death—about those who are cast into the lake of fire (see Revelation 20:14–15; 21:8). This truth is put succinctly into an interesting couplet I would ask you to write upon the tablet of your mind: "Born once, die twice. Born twice, die once." We will experience either the second birth or the second death. There is no other choice.

Prayer: O God, forgive us our hard hearts.
Forgive us our cold hearts. Forgive us our
little love for You. Jesus, give us the grace to wonder
anew at what You have done on the cross.

"The Son of God became a man to
enable men to become sons of God."
(C. S. Lewis)

SINLESS SAVIOR

Can any of you prove me guilty of sin?

One of the key points of the cross is that Christ was the perfect sacrifice. He was the Lamb without blemish or stain.

At Christmastime we sing, "O Holy Night… It is the night of our dear Savior's birth." Have you ever considered how appropriate nighttime is for the Savior to be born? Nighttime—the nurse of devout affections, the father of holy meditations, the wellspring of our deepest aspirations. Nighttime—how opposite a time for the Light of the World to come in to this earth.

And how glorious a time it was for those first shepherds. They were so familiar with the night, as they often spent the entire night keeping watch over their flocks in the valleys and the hills around the little town of Bethlehem. Suddenly they were surrounded by the brightness of noon, by the effulgent glory, the Shekinah glory of God. The same glory that had shone upon the mountain when Moses received the law. The same glory that was seen over the Holy of Holies in the Tabernacle. It was the brightness of the presence of God.

The shepherds heard the voices of a multitude of angels singing. Then the glorious announcement was made: "Fear not: for, behold, I bring you good tidings of great joy" (Luke 2:10, KJV).

Isn't it interesting that when God first came and sent His angel to bring those messages, the first words the angel spoke were, "Fear not"? Did we have reason to fear?

Well, Adam thought so after he sinned. When he heard the voice of God as he and Eve were walking in the Garden, they hid themselves among the trees because they knew they were guilty.

DID YOU KNOW?
The central message of the Bible is not good advice; it is Good News. The very word *gospel* itself (*evangelian* in Greek) means "glad tidings" or "good news." The good news is that even though we haven't kept His good advice in His law and His commandments, God loves us and will receive us still. What wonderful tidings those are indeed: "For there is born to you this day in the city of David a Savior, who is Christ the Lord" (Luke 2:11).

Many on that first Christmas night—and many today—did not and do not know that the tiny baby-thing on His mother's breast was the great Creator of the universe. The architect of eternity come now to clothe Himself in human flesh, that He might live in our midst to be our Savior.

People suppose Jesus was merely a teacher and merely a great example. But we need a Savior, not merely an example.

Dr. Joseph Parker once returned home from a concert where he heard the magnificent and incomparable Paderewski play the piano. As he came into his own room and looked at his piano, he was moved to close the lid and never touch it again—so overwhelmed was he by the example of Paderewski.

And so overwhelming is the example of Jesus Christ. The peerless Christ. The crystal Christ. The sinless One. Though we may look good compared to some of our neighbors, when we stand up before the full glory of Jesus, we see ourselves in all our littleness and pettiness and vileness and uncleanliness. We know ourselves to be unclean in the presence of His purity.

No, what we most need is a Savior. That's the great need of

the heart. A Savior to cleanse us and redeem us and to lift us up and to renew us and to grant us life eternal.

Many people who aren't Christians are quite willing to go along with celebrating Christmas. It's nice to have a little inspiration—a time of good cheer, a sharing of gifts, brotherly love. All of this is nice. But they aren't willing to celebrate Easter—and certainly not Good Friday. A Savior—now, that's a different thing from good cheer and brotherly love. After all, who needs a Savior? Only one type of person. The person who is lost—just as the person who needs a teacher is the person who is ignorant, and the person who needs a physician is the person who's sick.

Only a sinless Savior—only *the* sinless Savior—could pay the acceptable price. If Jesus were not perfect, if He were flawed in any way, His sacrifice on the cross would not have been sufficient to pay for our sins.

Prayer: Jesus, thank You that You and You alone lived a perfect life so that Your sacrifice on the cross would be sufficient for all who come to You.

"The world doesn't want Christ, but it needs Him." (Earle Stevens)

21

CHRIST'S BITTER CUP

O My Father, if it is possible, let this cup pass from Me;
nevertheless, not as I will, but as You will.

JESUS, IN MATTHEW 26:39

In the Garden of Gethsemane, Christ cries out to His Father, "O My Father, if it is possible, let this cup pass from Me" (Matthew 26:39). Can this be the mighty Son of God who stilled the stormy sea and calmed the winds, who now cries out in anguish?

What was in that mysterious cup that appeared before Christ's face there in the darkness of Gethsemane?

In that cup was *sin*—all the sin of the world.

Imagine you're visiting the Centers for Disease Control in Atlanta. You go into a large sealed room and see hundreds of beakers which you're told contain the distillation of the germs, the bacteria, and the viruses for all the most dangerous diseases known to mankind, from the black plague and leprosy to cancer and AIDS, and every foul disease man has ever known. There you see a technician who is one by one pouring the cultures of each vial into a large beaker. In that beaker is the accumulation of all the deadly diseases facing humankind.

Would it not be our tendency to shrink back farther and farther from that horror, that beaker of death that now stands before us? If you were asked to touch it, you would recoil with terror. Should you be told that you must drink its contents, the most unimaginable dread and fear would fill your soul.

Yet that is as nothing compared to what Jesus saw that dark night in Gethsemane when He saw before Him all the sin of the world.

I once saw a film in which a man stepped inside a small hut not knowing who or what was inside, and there in a dimly lit room he found himself face-to-face with someone whose features were horribly distorted by what he immediately recognized as the dread disease of leprosy. Instantly he stepped back, and the desire to flee, to run as far and as fast as he could, almost overwhelmed him. Would not each of us do the same?

But can you imagine even more being trapped in such a small room with a dozen or more lepers all around you, reaching out and touching you, handling your hands, breathing in your face? Would you not recoil with the utmost horror? For one who isn't a leper, it would be more horrible than we could possibly describe. However, if you *were* a leper, you would not recoil; leprosy would simply be something you live with and handle daily.

Likewise, we do not recoil from the horror of sin because *we* are the sinners; we are in the midst of sin daily. It is touching us. We handle it daily. We participate in it—sometimes joyfully. It is part of our lives.

That isn't true for Jesus, the undefiled One, the Pure One, the Paragon of Virtue. What horror and dread filled His soul as He looked in that cup filled with sin.

However, there was more than sin in the cup. Jesus had said (in effect), "You all shall go away and forsake me and leave me alone. But I am not alone, for my Father is with me." How He delighted to say, "Father...I know

The Great Exchange: a cup of death in exchange for a cup of life. Christ emptied the bitter cup, so that He could extend to us the Communion cup.

that You always hear Me" (John 11:41–42). Always He dwelt in the intimate communion of the presence of His Father's love. But now He looked into this cup and saw there all the sins of the world:

All of the sin since first Cain smashed the brains of his brother Abel.

All the sins of Auschwitz and the Gulag Archipelago.

All of the vile sins of blasphemy and profanity.

All of the vile sins of fornication and adultery and sodomy and lesbianism.

All of the sins of the flesh.

All of the anger and hatred.

All of the jealousy and the lust and greed.

All this was squeezed and distilled in that singular cup.

As bad as this was, there was more than the sin of the world in that bitter cup. There was also to be found there the dreaded abandonment by God—abandonment by the One who can not tolerate sin. On our behalf, God made Jesus to *be* sin—"He made Him who knew no sin to be sin for us" (2 Corinthians 5:21).

As the time came for His death, Jesus began to feel the worm of sin in the very marrow of His bones. Sin was poured out upon His very body and soul. Jesus Christ, the pure, spotless Son of God, became the greatest sinner who ever lived. All the guilt of the world was piled upon Him. Christ became the arch-criminal of the universe. God looked down upon His beloved Son and saw sin and therefore turned His back on Him. Jesus was abandoned by His Father.

"My God, My God, why have You forsaken Me?" (Matthew 27:46). Ah, look within yourself and see the guilt of man's iniquity, and the answer to that question is clear. He was forsaken by God and abandoned by His Father. There He hung, quivering with all the loathsomeness and vileness of sin—alone and abandoned by God.

Prayer: Lord Jesus Christ, You were abandoned,
so we do not have to be abandoned. You were alone
on the cross, so that we can be together with You now
and in heaven. Make us eternally grateful.

"When the cup of our wickedness was filled, when it had become quite clear that as its reward we were to expect punishment and death...then—oh, overflowing kindness and love of God!—then he did not hate us or reject us.... In his compassion he took our sins upon himself." (Justin Martyr)

22

VIA DOLOROSA

*And when they had mocked Him, they took
the robe off Him, put His own clothes on Him,
and led Him away to be crucified.*

MATTHEW 27:31

Christ is the touchstone of character. What we really are in
the depths of our souls is revealed by our encounter with
Him. I remember a lovely lady who often waited upon my wife
and me when we visited a certain store. She was a pure delight.
She was lovely of face and figure and had a marvelous personality. She was exceedingly gracious and yet dignified and friendly
and warm. One day my wife, while visiting the store, entered
into a conversation with this lady and brought up the subject of
Christ and her relationship to Him.

In relating this incident to me, my wife said, "The strangest
thing happened. This woman seemed to be transfigured before
my eyes, and her countenance was changed. She became glar-
ingly opposed to all I was saying." The lady's true nature was
revealed—because Christ is the touchstone of the real character
of our soul.

In the final scene in the great drama of the life and death of
Jesus Christ, many come into contact with Christ and have their
deepest selves revealed. They appear ostensibly to judge and
condemn Christ. But, in actuality, they come to be irradiated by
the brilliant light emanating from the Son of God. They have
revealed the depths of their own soul—the real nature of their

own character—so they indeed might be tried and judged, and either condemned or acquitted.

Here we see the Pharisees, who hounded the steps of Jesus throughout His ministry. Here are the Sadducees, as well as the high priests and the Sanhedrin. Here we find Pilate, the Roman governor, as well as Herod, the dilapidated and dissipated king of Galilee. Here we find Peter the denier; Judas the apostate; Annas the wily old ecclesiastical politician; and Caiaphas, who conceived the whole horrid plot in his own depraved mind. They're all here for one final reprise on the stage of history in the drama of the ages on the Via Dolorosa—that is, the dolorous way, the way of sorrows, the way of suffering, the way of grief, the way of pain.

Most specifically, the Via Dolorosa stretched from the praetorium of Pilate to the hill of Golgotha. But in a larger sense, that dolorous way began when Christ left the ivory palaces of paradise and stepped down into the stench of a filthy stable to be born of a woman, to be born under the law, to be born as our substitute. For Jesus, all of this way was a Via Dolorosa. He was indeed "a Man of sorrows and acquainted with grief" (Isaiah 53:3). He came to suffer that we might rejoice.

As the witnesses accused Jesus, what was His response?

Jesus was silent. Why was Jesus silent? Sometimes a person is silent because he is giving tacit consent to what is being spoken by others. Could this be the case with Jesus here? Many accusations were made against Him, and yet He denied none of them. Was He perchance guilty?

In the answer to that lies the very heart of the Christian faith. We must uncompromisingly declare that Jesus Christ was silent precisely because He *was guilty*. He was guilty of everything with which He was charged, and He was guilty of many crimes for which He was not charged. He was guiltier than any man who had ever stood before the Sanhedrin. He was guiltier than the vilest miscreant who shall ever stand before the judgment bar of God. He was the guiltiest man who ever lived…but the guilt He bore was not His own. It was yours and it was mine. "The LORD has laid on Him the iniquity of us all" (Isaiah 53:6).

God made Him to *be sin* for us. Guilty—as charged.

Did the Jews crucify Christ? Remember the controversy surrounding Mel Gibson's movie *The Passion*? Based on some of the charges made, one would think this film was going to reopen the scab of soured Judeo-Christian relations and cause some new pogrom. There's no question that inexcusable atrocities have been perpetuated against the Jews through the ages by so-called Christians who have used the death of Christ as an excuse for venting their anti-Semitism. But such a pogrom has *never* happened in countries where evangelicalism is a major player. In the wake of Mel Gibson's film, there was no anti-Semitic flare-up. Nothing—although I can't recall that the *New York Times* apologized to Mel Gibson for their dire and utterly false predictions.

> Who killed Jesus? It was actually God the Father who ultimately put Jesus Christ to death. It was His plan and His will for His good purposes.

So I raise the question again—did the Jews crucify Christ? There can be no question of the fact that the plot was conceived by Caiaphas, the high priest. It was carried out by the Sanhedrin, with the help of Judas. But that isn't all of the answer. The Romans, as Gentiles, actually carried out His crucifixion, so we may say that it was the Jews *and* the Romans who killed Him.

However, if we do that, we still will have missed the point. The wider truth is that all of us were involved in His death. It was because of *our* sins that He died.

So who killed Christ?

It was Mother Teresa who placed that thorny crown upon His head.

It was Billy Graham who hammered in those nails.

It was Francis Schaeffer who placed the occupied cross in its place on Calvary.

It was you.

It was me.

And yet even here Jesus takes responsibility—for He boldly declared, "*I lay down my life* that I may take it again. *No one takes it from Me*, but I lay it down of Myself. I have power to lay it down, and I have power to take it again" (John 10:17–18).

Prayer: Thank You, Jesus, for laying down Your life for us—for submitting to the Father's will. By the power of the Holy Spirit, help us to submit to Your will today.

"The perfect surrender and humiliation were undergone by Christ: perfect because He was God, surrender and humiliation because He was man."
(C. S. Lewis)

23

A MEDICAL DOCTOR EXAMINES CHRIST'S SUFFERINGS

Joseph took the body, wrapped it in a clean linen cloth,
and placed it in his own new tomb that he had cut out of the rock.
MATTHEW 27:59–60, NIV

W hat does a medical doctor have to say about the sufferings of Christ, culminating in the Crucifixion? In this
chapter and the next we'll explore this question. (This chapter
will deal with the Shroud per se, the scourging and the crown of
thorns. The next chapter will deal with the Crucifixion itself.)

Dr. Alan Whanger, a retired professor from Duke Medical
Center, has spent his life studying medicine. In addition, since the
late 1970s, he has studied intensely the Shroud of Turin, a fourteen-
foot-long by three-foot-wide linen cloth, which he is convinced is
the burial cloth of Jesus Christ. Although the Shroud was dis-
missed by some as a fake because of the carbon dating in 1988
of a single specimen (divided into three tiny parts) that was said
to date from AD 1260 to 1390, Dr. Whanger says this test was not
valid. He and his wife, Mary (coauthor with him of the book *The
Shroud of Turin: An Adventure of Discovery*), say that the problem
wasn't with the dating per se; it was with the sample, which came
from the very corner of the cloth, a part rewoven in the Middle
Ages. And so he concludes that the carbon dating "was totally
invalid and has no scientific merit."

Furthermore, Dr. Whanger notes, "The Shroud is the most intensely studied single object in existence. There are probably 67 different fields of scientific and academic interests that have looked into the Shroud in one way or another. So, there's been a huge amount of research….

"It is our convic-
tion," he continues,
"that the Shroud is,
indeed, the burial
cloth of Jesus of
Nazareth. And we feel that we can date it to the spring of A.D. 30 in the Middle East, and that what we see on the Shroud with the various wounds is that this is entirely consistent with the Scriptural account of the crucifixion of Jesus. And traditionally, this has been known as the image of Jesus."

"I love Thee because Thou has first loved me
And purchased my pardon on Calvary's tree.
I love Thee for wearing the thorns on Thy brow.
If ever I loved Thee, My Jesus, 'tis now."
(A. J. Gordon)

In other words, observes Dr. Whanger, what we think Jesus looked like is based on the Shroud of Turin, and not vice versa.

In a recent interview, Dr. Whanger commented on the sufferings of Jesus as seen in the Shroud.

"We can see incredible detail on the Shroud. First, we see that He was severely beaten. We can see that the right eye is swollen shut, that actually the nose has been dislocated, the right eye is swollen shut, and there are bruises—not only on the face, but we can see bruises across the shoulders, as well. Even far worse, we have clear evidence that He was scourged in a terrible fashion as He was hit with these Roman whips, which were leather straps with metal dumbbells on them with little barbs on them. So, whenever He was hit, it would drive these barbs into the flesh, and when the scourge was pulled back, they would tear little bits of the flesh. We can see on the Shroud that He was hit about 125 times front and back with these scourges, which had basically turned Him into a pathetic bloody mass.

"Mel Gibson was aware of the Shroud, so that actually he based the scourging in *The Passion of the Christ* on what we see on the Shroud. To do this type of scourging would have taken 20–25 minutes. It was a terrible bloody mess. It would have half-killed any individual beaten this way.

"Again, they often embedded little pieces of lead or metal at the end of these whips. Or they would take sometimes sheep knucklebones, which were kind of rough and irregular and put them along the edges in order to tear out bits and pieces of the flesh with each lash.

"They could easily kill a person doing that. But Jesus was young and strong. On the front of the Shroud showing the chest area, we can see the scourge marks, but they carefully would avoid hitting Him over the heart, which could have killed Him on the spot. So, they were not trying to kill Him. This was obviously done by professional scourgers, whose job it was to beat people. We can tell from the pattern of the scourge marks that there were two of these lictors—these were the Roman soldiers who beat people—who were doing this. They were, obviously, pros at doing this; and so, they just lacerated him from head to foot, front and back on each side. A person getting scourged like this may have not survived this for a long period of time, but they were not trying to kill Him. They were trying to keep Him alive because they wanted to get the victims out to crucify them. They didn't want to kill them down in the police headquarters or the army headquarters.

"As to the Crown of Thorns: As we studied the Shroud, we saw evidence of thistles. We find on there images of other objects [such as what would have come into contact with Him—i.e., the nails, the hammer, the spear, the sponge on a stick, etc.], along with the image of the crucified man. Included there are the images of many flowers and plants and even thistles, such as *Gundelia tournefortii*. We can see on the Shroud the Crown of

Thorns placed near the body. There are still remnants of some of the thorns sticking in the back of the head."

*Prayer: Lord Jesus, we cannot fathom
the depth of Your sufferings for us.
But we thank You and pray that if ever our love for
You grows cold, You will again show us Your cross.*

"To try to interpret [the Shroud of Turin] as the product of some unknown medieval faker seems rather like arguing for the Taj Mahal being a mere geological accident." (Ian Wilson)

A MEDICAL DOCTOR EXAMINES THE CRUCIFIXION

*Pilate marveled that He was already dead; and summoning
the centurion, he asked him if He had been dead for some time.*

MARK 15:44

I n this chapter, Dr. Alan Whanger continues his medical exam-
ination of the cross as evidenced by the Shroud of Turin. Here
are his further observations specifically on the Crucifixion itself:

"We can see the nail wound in the left wrist quite plainly,
and it is plainly in the wrist and not in the palm of the hand as
seen in many artistic depictions with the nail wound in the palm
of the hand. But that tissue is not strong enough to hold the body
up, which, of course, the Romans, who did thousands of crucifixions, knew. And so they knew where to put the nail through
the wrist so with one blow they could put the half-inch thick nail
right through the wrist without breaking anything.

"We think when the nails were put through, they damaged
the median nerve, running through the wrist, and damaging the
nerve causes intense spasm, which is extraordinarily painful. So,
we think that the thumbs were actually pulled into the palms.

"This type of crucifixion was probably the worst type of punishment ever devised—not only all the preliminaries, the beating
and the scourging and so forth. But this type of crucifixion was
sort of a slow agonizing death—between the terrible pain coming

from the nails being put through, hitting the major nerves in the body, and the suffocation. The individual would tend to slump forward, particularly after they got weaker from all this terrible ordeal, and it is hard to breathe. And so, the individual would struggle to get his breath out. And it was difficult—He had to kind of struggle to get breath back in, because it had been forced out. But, of course, they would soon faint from all the beating and the pain and so forth, and so this was sort of a slow writhing between this agonizing pain and suffocation, until the individual mercifully died. Or when it got time for the executioner to go home, they would break the lower legs, so he could no longer push himself up, and he'd suffocate in probably 12 to 15 minutes.

Dr. Alan Whanger comments on the spear wound:
"We can see very plainly on the Shroud, in between the fourth and fifth rib on the right anterior chest wall, the spear wound, which is about an inch and a half in width. We can see a dark material coming out of this, which tests out to be human blood type AB, and we can see clear fluid, which has been tested out as human *serum albumen* [which looked like water]. This is, undoubtedly, the fluid that was in the lung cavity that the spear went through. Since the image of the spear is on the Shroud, we can tell the type of spear and the length of the head. And by comparing the length of the head of the spear with the spear wound, we can see very clearly that this spear hit the right side of the heart, which would have produced death in a living individual in a matter of seconds."

"So it was an awful form of execution. Of course, the Romans utilized that to show what happened to criminals or what happened to people who intended to threaten Rome. And they would use this as an example to warn people—you didn't cross Rome.

"And they would do the crucifixion in public, generally outside the city wall, and they would put the title (the titular) on each cross. The title had the person's name and the crime for which they were being crucified fastened to the cross. And they were out for public viewing.

"Now, in Israel, the Israelites did not want bodies left out after sundown. But in most parts of the Roman Empire, they would just tie the individuals to the cross, and they would just let them die of starvation and so forth over three or four days.

"When I look at the backside of the corpse on the Shroud, the body is in intense spasm. It's in a type of rigor mortis where an individual's been severely traumatized just before death. This is called cadaveric spasm. It's a type of rigor mortis that occurs almost instantly after death, so that the individual on the Shroud is in basically the same position He was in on the cross."

We asked Dr. Whanger what he would have listed as the single most significant cause of death, if he were writing the coroner's report for this body.

His answer: "The primary cause of death is awful trauma…from the scourging and the beating and all the rigors of the crucifixion. So, basically, shock, which would have been associated with blood loss and severe trauma. We think that, probably, a secondary feature—and we can get some inkling from this because it appears as though the ribcage is expanded—probably, some degree of suffocation. But we think the main problem was that He had just been beaten half to death and the blood loss finished it off."

Prayer: We marvel, Lord Jesus Christ,
Creator of the universe, that You would submit
Yourself to the abuse of sinful man in order to save us.

"These thousands of painful shocks [of Christ's passion] add up and multiply, each one increasing the sensitivity of the nervous system." (Pierre Barbet, MD)

25

THE DIVINE DRAMA

Now I saw heaven opened, and behold, a white horse.
And He who sat on him was called Faithful and True,
and in righteousness He judges and makes war.

REVELATION 19:11

The Son of God had gone forth to war. He had begun a great campaign. Single-handedly He would take on the demons of hell, the devil himself, and all the viciousness and wickedness of man. All of this He took on Himself. He had traveled far, suffered much, waited long for that great day—which was the consummation of it all.

This journey had begun in the counsels of the Trinity, long before the blackness of the skies broke out in scintillating galaxies and coruscating stars at the beginning of creation. Long before the foundations of the mountains were set, the decision was made in the counsels of the Triune God that Jesus Christ, the second Person of the Trinity, the Creator of the universe, the great Logos, the Son, would take upon Himself human flesh and depart from heaven. This would take Him out of the porphyry palaces of paradise and down into the poisonous prison of pain and sin and grief and woe.

He had come a long way. Throughout the eons of centuries preceding the creation of this world, there loomed always before Him this great consummation, this culmination day, this final destiny, His ultimate destination. It was the Omega point, the great final act of the greatest drama the world has ever seen.

At last, on this day He saw it, albeit only dimly. Through eyes clouded with sweat and blood, He saw it. Having collapsed there at the gate of Jerusalem, His back flailed open by the Roman whip, being crushed by the cross that now lay upon Him, He lifted up His head and there perchance for the first time He saw it: Golgotha, the place of a skull, the place of death—the great goal of His life.

At last He approached it. He staggered to His feet and began the final few steps. He had dragged this cross about 750 yards across the cobblestones of Jerusalem. Now He had come to this final destination of His life—the place, the time, the activity, the reason for which He had come.

As He lifted up His head, He could see on the precipitant face of a hill, blackened by the blood of thousands of criminals who had died there before, those strange concavities that clearly mark out the lineaments of a skull. He saw deep dark eyes, a place for a nose, the crooked mouth, the shape of the skull.

The divine drama came to a head on this hill. It was the Atonement of Christ, the most amazing thing that has ever been accomplished in this world.

DID YOU KNOW?

Atonement is a fascinating word. It is cobbled together out of pieces and little things. In actuality it comes from several words and parts which were put together: "at-one-ment." Atonement, where man—who is alienated from God—is reconciled to God and has peace in his heart. "Therefore, having been justified by faith, we have peace with God through our Lord Jesus Christ" (Romans 5:1).

He came to defeat the works of the devil. At the cross, Jesus seemed to be defeated. In reality, He was the victor, despoiling the devil's schemes.

For Christ, the cross was the *terminus ad quem*, the point toward which His entire life was moving. For us, it is the opposite. It is the *terminus a quo*, the point from which all of our life emanates. When we come to the cross, our Christian life begins, and we go forth in His name as soldiers of the cross.

Many decades ago, a wealthy man in Chicago had a son who contracted some kind of rare fever, and it was written up in the local newspapers. It was feared the boy might die, and the father made arrangements to bring in a specialist all the way from India to try to heal his boy.

Someone on the street, in reading the newspaper and talking about this, said to his friend, "Just what is it the boy has?"

His friend answered, "I don't know exactly what he has, but it must be terribly serious, seeing how far the physician is being brought to try to heal him."

How far did Christ have to come? He had to leave the glories of heaven to come to earth for our sake.

---

*Prayer: Father, be with us as we contemplate
the cross, and show us the awfulness of our sin
that we might behold the glory of the cross.*

"O cross, tool of salvation of the
most high! O cross, banner of
Christ's victory over all enemies!"
(Attributed to Saint Andrew)

THE CONQUEST
OF SATAN

For this purpose the Son of God was manifested,
that He might destroy the works of the devil.
1 JOHN 3:8

Satan! What do you know about him? Do you believe he exists?

Did you realize he runs a travel agency? He has the largest travel agency in the world, and he has taken many people on a great journey.

Before you sign up too quickly for such a journey, you might want to remember that he may take you further than you want to go and keep you longer than you want to stay and charge you more than you want to pay. He is a most malevolent individual, and we should be aware of him.

Christ left heaven and came to this earth and became flesh and blood to destroy both Satan and his works. In spite of that, you still hear people say, "Oh, I don't believe in the devil." I'm sure you've heard people say that. You might want to reply, "Oh, really? Then, obviously you don't believe in God, because God tells us there definitely is a devil. And evidently you don't believe in God's Word, because it repeatedly states this to be true. Furthermore, you obviously don't believe in Christ, because He was tempted by Satan, He talked to him, and He did mortal combat with him at the cross." Indeed, to deny the reality of Satan is to challenge, ultimately, the very essence of the Christian faith.

Who is Satan? Where did he come from?

He is an angel—an angel who sinned. Before he sinned, his name was Lucifer, meaning the "light-bearer." Lucifer was the mightiest, the most beautiful, the most powerful of all God's angels. He sinned, we're told in both Isaiah 14 and Ezekiel 28. The image of Satan looms up beyond the description of any earthly tyrants, because no human tyrant was ever in heaven or in the Garden to tempt our first parents.

> The Bible tells us Christ came to destroy Satan—as well as Satan's works. "For this purpose the Son of God was manifested, that He might destroy the works of the devil" (1 John 3:8). Indeed, He came to do both, and He will first destroy his works and ultimately destroy him. The term *destroy* in this passage doesn't mean "to annihilate" but rather "to render ineffectual"—to render Satan's works impotent, to cause his works to cease to be any kind of an active and dangerous threat in the world.

What was the nature of Lucifer's sin? It was simply one thought—not an act, not even a word—but a thought to himself when he said in his own heart, "I will be God." He was thrown out of heaven and took with him a great host of other angels. They're collectively known today as demons. Satan, or the devil, is simply the leader of these. Like them, he is a fallen angel. Therefore, he is not infinite. He is not omnipotent. He is not omnipresent. He is not everywhere.

But he is extremely powerful nonetheless. We are no match, *nolo contendre*. It is no battle at all, except for the fact that we are in Christ, and Jesus is more than conqueror and more than capable of delivering us from Satan.

A man and his two little boys were walking in the woods one day when a huge bumblebee came and stung the older one on the arm. His father rushed to his rescue. Then the bee began to buzz around the head of the other brother, who fell to the ground and was kicking and screaming and waving his arms and trying to get the bee away. His father calmly said to him, "Bobby, don't be afraid; it can't hurt you; it left its stinger in Johnny!"

Likewise Satan has left his stinger in Christ, and those who are His and are in Him cannot be hurt by Satan. So we need not fear him, and certainly we should not believe anything he says, because he is a liar from the beginning.

Therefore, resist him and overcome him. How do we do that? We do it by the power of His blood and by our testimony, we're told by John. By the cross of Christ, where Satan was defeated. It is only in the blood of Christ and by the power of Christ that we can overcome him. In His glorious name, and in our testimony, which declares that we're taking hold of the cross, we are saying, "Be gone, Satan, and leave me alone." Then you will discover that this being, capable (as angels are) of killing 185,000 soldiers in one night (see 2 Kings 19:35 or Isaiah 37:36), will depart. Just that simply.

Christ came to destroy his works and his person, and He has given us the power of His cross, His armor, His Word, His blood, and our testimony to those things by which we can resist the devil. And we're told and assured that he will flee from us.

Prayer: Praise be to You, Lord Jesus Christ,
for conquering our archenemy and making a spectacle of
him on the cross. Thank You that Your victory is our victory.

"You can see that the crucified Christ
possesses the hidden power of God:
Every demon, in fact all and every
power and authority on earth, trembles
before him." (Justin Martyr)

27

THE WARFARE
WITHIN

And do not lead us into temptation,
but deliver us from the evil one.

MATTHEW 6:13

B y the power of the cross, we're set free from the power of sin. Therefore, we can pray—with confidence and expectation—that we not be led into temptation and that we be delivered from the evil one. Although millions still pray, "Deliver us from evil," the best translation from the Greek is that which we find above—deliver us from the evil one. That is, deliver us from Satan.

Paul talks about spiritual warfare in the seventh chapter of Romans: "For the good that I will to do, I do not do; but the evil I will not to do, that I practice" (v. 19). He says he sees a principle of warfare within him, bringing him into captivity. That warfare is brought about by the new birth. For in the new birth, Jesus Christ comes to live in our hearts and creates within us an entirely new nature. The Scripture says, "Therefore, if anyone is in Christ, he is a new creation; old things have passed away; behold, all things have become new" (2 Corinthians 5:17). This means we have a new spiritual nature created within us—we have been born from above.

The new birth creates a new nature that is perfectly sinless and is not capable of sinning. The new nature then dwells within us with the old nature. That old nature isn't capable of doing good; it can do nothing but sin. That sin may be a very "respectable" sin or it may be that of a drunkard, a wino in an alley. It may be that of the president of a great corporation or the mayor of a city. But it's still sin.

Both of these natures living within the Christian create this struggle, this warfare within. Paul says he sees these two natures warring within himself. We have within us, as it were, a Dr. Jekyll and Mr. Hyde. Someone has said that Dr. Jekyll was attempting to rid himself of his evil nature; instead, he rid himself of his good nature, and what was left was vile and hideous.

As a young man, Augustine prayed to this effect: "Lord, make me sexually pure—but not yet!" An exact translation of his unorthodox prayer is: "Give me chastity and continence, but not yet!"

In the fourth century, Augustine described well the warfare within:

> The enemy had control of my will, and out of it he fashioned a chain and fettered me with it. For in truth lust is made out of a perverse will, and when lust is served, it becomes habit, and when habit is not resisted, it becomes necessity. By such links, joined one to another, as it were—for this reason I have called it a chain—a harsh bondage held me fast. A new will, which had begun within me, to wish freely to worship you and find joy in you, O God, the sole sure delight, was not yet able to overcome that prior will, grown strong with age. Thus did my two wills, the one old, the other new, the first carnal, and the second spiritual, contend with one another, and by their conflict they laid waste my soul.

Augustine also declared: "Unhappy man that I was! Who would deliver me from the body of this death, unless your grace through Jesus Christ our Lord?" Christ was the key to victory for Augustine's soul. Today we even call him "*Saint* Augustine"— although he would be the first to admit he was a sinner.

In fact, when Christ comes into a person's life, that person is the one who most sees himself to be a sinner. The fact of the matter is that though he is becoming better, his eyesight is improving, and he sees himself as more and more sinful. Those natures never change. The old nature does not become better; it may be mortified, but it is still there. It is still "Mr. Hyde," ready to lurch out of the shadows and do ill. It's like a wild, untamed animal that, although chained, still has its fangs and its claws. And if it breaks loose, it can do great damage.

Bill Bright used to tell a story that described the old and new natures as two dogs: a black dog and a white dog that were wont to fight viciously. "Which dog will win," he said, "is determined by which dog you feed. Feed the black dog and starve the white dog, and the black dog will win; feed the white dog and starve the black dog, and the white dog will win."

Which nature are you feeding? You may be feeding your old and sin-filled nature depending on what you watch on television, or what movies you see, or what books you read. Take pornography as an example. By consuming it, whether on the Internet or in magazines or videos, you're inflaming the passions of the old nature and starving the new. If you constantly feed the old nature, is there any question of how this warfare will end?

How much feeding are you doing to the new nature within? Do you spend time in the Word of God? Do you have a quiet time when you read it, where you study it, where you meditate upon it, where you hide it in your heart? Do you have a time of prayer to God to confess your sins, to seek the infilling of His Spirit, to seek the guidance only He can give and the powers only He can grant? Do you seek Him every day? Feed the new nature, and watch God bless you immensely.

Prayer: Oh, Lord, through the power
of Your Holy Spirit, please deliver me from
the wiles and schemes of the evil one.
Thank You that You crushed his power on the cross.

"Two natures beat within my breast.
The one is foul, the other blessed.
The one I love, the other I hate.
The one I feed will dominate."
(Anonymous)

28

THE CONQUEST OF THE CONQUERED

When He ascended on high, He led captivity captive,
and gave gifts to men.

EPHESIANS 4:8

The title of this chapter, "The Conquest of the Conquered," is rather enigmatic, but it contains wrapped within it a great spiritual truth which is vital for each one of us to understand. Perhaps it is enigmatic because it comes out of this rather mysterious text quoted above. Jesus ascended to heaven, but first He descended into the lower parts of the earth.

First of all, let us see what the surface meaning of this text is. You may know that in the Old Testament, before Jesus Christ came, all those who died went to a place called, in the Hebrew, "Sheol." To this place of Sheol went both the wicked and the righteous. There have been those who have said that there were two compartments. Be that as it may, the Bible simply says that the wicked and the righteous went to Sheol. In this shadowy land, those who were believers waited for that great event, the promised coming of the Messiah.

When Jesus came into this world, He descended from His throne in glory and came down into the womb of Mary, then into the body of a little child. He came to the carpenter's bench. He came to the scorn of men. He came to the bitter agony of Gethsemane and Calvary, and on that great cataclysmic day, Jesus went to the cross. By His coming, He changed the whole course of human history in this world. But He was also to have a profound effect upon the world of spirits—that dark world beneath.

What does it mean to say Christ "led captivity captive"? To understand this, we need a little historical backdrop. In the Roman world, there occurred on occasion what was called a "triumph." It came on the heels of another successful Roman conquest. The triumph was a spectacle well known to every citizen of Rome. Tens of thousands of spectators would gather. On those occasions, when a great general would return, the army would gather outside the city and move through the triumphal arch on their way to the temple.

We don't have to wait until we die to experience the triumph; it is going on right now. God always leads us in triumph in Christ. This is a life-changing concept. Our Captain, our King, our General, has won the victory; He has conquered death; He has conquered hell; He has conquered all the forces of evil, and we partake of His victory—and even receive the spoils of His warfare.

First would come the trumpeters, sounding in thrilling tones the notes of victory. Behind the trumpeters would come great floats upon which had been erected portraits of the conquered cities—towers, walls, and all. Then would come rumbling by the wagons filled with the spoils of victory, followed by seventy white oxen walking philosophically to their death, to be offered in sacrifice to the gods. Behind the oxen came, in chains, the chieftains and captains of the armies of the enemy who, like the oxen, would soon meet their end. Then there were lictors, harpists, flutists, and those bearing incense. Great roars of victory went up.

Then came the general in a purple toga, with a golden crown upon his head, an ivory scepter in his hand, and a laurel branch—the insignia of victory. Behind his magnificent white chariot came the rest of the conquered, the army of the enemy, chained, and with their heads down. At last came the victorious army of Rome, each soldier wearing a crown. In the midst of the cries of the people, the sounds of the trumpets and the harpists, the fragrance of the incense, they made their way to the Temple of Jupiter.

This was a "triumph." Paul is telling us that Jesus Christ, the Captain of the well-fought fight, the greatest General of all times, has come and has had a greater victory than any of these. He has come, not only into the opposition and hostility of this world, but He has gone into the very portals of hell. There He has taken on the demons of the underworld, and now He leads a great triumphal victory into the metropolis of heaven. Behind Him come all the saints of Old Testament times and all those who have trusted in Him. This is the triumph.

Paul tells us, secondly, that this triumphal march, this triumphal entry into heaven, is still going on. The same apostle, in 2 Corinthians 2:14, says that God always leads us in triumph in Christ.

This triumphal march is going on right now, but it is somewhat different. You see, in the army of Christ, all the vanquished have enlisted, including those who were once enemies, such as Paul himself, who once opposed Christ and is now one of the leaders of that army. As we look at the triumph of Christ, we see the vanquished and the conquerors merge as one. The apostle Paul once went forth to war against Jesus, but he was struck to the ground outside Damascus, the sword was smitten from his hand, and he was conquered by the Son of Man. In that conquest Paul was to realize his greatest victory, and he, too, was to become a part of the ongoing triumph of Christ—a triumph that is even now proceeding into the heavenly city.

Prayer: Thank You, Jesus, for going to hell for our sake and freeing us from being captive to the evil one.

"Faith is a crusade—
no weaklings need apply."
(Henry M. Edmonds)

29

HE IS EXALTED

Therefore God also has highly exalted Him
and given Him the name which is above every name.

PHILIPPIANS 2:9

In Philippians 2 we find one of the most marvelous passages on the incarnation of Jesus Christ. In it Paul tells us that our attitude should be like that of Jesus, who, although He was God, humbled Himself and became a man. Jesus obeyed God the Father—even to the point of dying a shameful death.

Crucifixion was reserved for slaves and the lower classes in Rome. It was not allowed for Roman citizens, and certainly not for righteous or innocent men. The Roman historian Tacitus spoke of it as "a nefarious action...that is incapable of description by any word, for there is none fit to describe it."

Because Jesus humbled Himself in this way, God the Father has exalted Him forevermore.

We're reminded of the exalted name of Jesus every year at Christmastime. Everywhere in the world, whether they're conscious of it or not, hundreds of millions of people across the globe directly or indirectly pay Him homage at the time set aside to remember His birth.

Christmas is not only a special day—a very special day—in the truest meaning of the word; it is a *unique* day. There's nothing like it in all the world. If somehow we could be lifted high enough to see what was happening in every house in our nation on Christmas Eve and Christmas Day, we would discover that in virtually every single city, in every town, in every village, in every hamlet in America, there would be people worshiping Jesus Christ.

"Alexander, Caesar, Charlemagne, and I founded great empires. But upon what did the creation of our genius depend? Upon force. Jesus alone founded his empire upon love, and to this very day millions would die for him." (Napoleon Bonaparte)

But that isn't merely the province of this country. If you traveled south through Central America and South America, all the way down to Patagonia, you would find men and women worshiping Christ in every nation and in every city. Travel east to the continent of Europe and all of its nations, south into Algeria, Morocco, Sierra Leone, Madagascar, and all the nations of Africa without exception, and you would find people bowing the knee and worshiping by the tens of millions the Lord Jesus Christ. In fact, you would find more people worshiping Christ in Africa than you would in North America; in fact, you would find more people worshiping Christ in Africa than you would find *people* in North America.

Travel westward across the vast expanse of Asia down into Australia, Tasmania, New Zealand, Borneo, Irian Jaya, the Solomon Islands, Vanuatu, and all the other thousands of islands in the Pacific. You will not find one where Christ is not adored.

Christ is the greatest Man who ever lived on this planet; of that there isn't the slightest doubt. This truth is absolutely astonishing when you consider that He was cut off in His young manhood at thirty-three years of age. Plato was just a budding philosopher at thirty-three. Many of the great writers were far older than that before they wrote anything of significance. And so it could be said of many statesmen and other great people of the world.

Yet before Jesus would even fully mature, by our standards, He was cut off as a malefactor, crucified between thieves, and abandoned by His followers. He wrote no books, and yet the books written about Him would fill the largest library in the world. He wrote no music, and yet more songs, more oratorios, more anthems, more hymns have been written about Him than about anyone who ever lived.

Already the number of those serving Him is twice the size of any other competing religion, and the number is growing much faster. His church in all its multiple facets is the greatest phenomenon this planet has ever seen. It is the everlasting kingdom of our Lord and Savior Jesus Christ, the greatest Person who ever walked upon this planet.

Philip Schaff, a Yale professor from the nineteenth century and prolific church historian, says it all: "This Jesus of Nazareth, without money and arms, conquered more millions than Alexander, Caesar, Mohammed, and Napoleon; without science and learning, He shed more light on all things human and divine than all philosophers and scholars combined.... He set more pens in motion...than the whole army of great men of ancient and modern times."

Prayer: Lord Jesus Christ, we praise You
for humbling Yourself for our salvation's sake.
Therefore, You are exalted above all.

"I am an historian. I am not a believer, but I must confess as a historian that this penniless preacher from Nazareth is irrevocably the very center of history. Jesus Christ is easily the most dominant figure in all history." (H. G. Wells)

WHY BE THANKFUL?

But thanks be to God, who gives us the victory
through our Lord Jesus Christ.
1 CORINTHIANS 15:57, ESV

We should be perpetually grateful when we think of the cross. Yet most of us think of gratitude as sort of a little something extra special. It would be nice if we had it, but it's not really part of the essence of the Christian life or the Christian faith.

Well, may I say that the Bible talks about gratitude scores of times, far more than many subjects we think to be very important? In fact, I think we could safely say that no ungrateful person will ever end up in heaven. Think about that.

I think many people fail to realize the connection between thankfulness and prayer. If we look at some of the things the Bible says about thankfulness, we discover these words: "Rejoice always, pray without ceasing, in everything give thanks" (1 Thessalonians 5:16–18). I wonder if you noticed the order? Rejoice, pray, give thanks. Joyful praise and giving of thanks are the two wings, as it were, for praying successfully and unceasingly.

Many people feel that their prayers never get past the ceiling; but just bounce off. This could be because they're trying to fly, so to speak, with their wings clipped.

Some large birds raised for commercial purposes are no longer kept inside in cages, but are let out into large pens that have about five- or six-foot fences. The birds there are free to roam and fly away—if they could. But you see, they have had their wings clipped. They might run into that fence a number of times before they discover the folly of it, and they learn to live happily, I suppose, within the boundaries of that large pen.

But they were created for more than that, and so are we in our prayers. The wing of rejoicing praise and the wing of giving thanks are the powerful pinions of prayers that lift our petitions up to the throne of God.

Of course, rejoicing praise means being thankful to God for *who He is*—for His greatness, His glory, His power, His omnipotence, and His omniscience. Thankfulness means thanking God for *what He has done*—His grace, the salvation He accomplished for us at such at a terrible price. By His cross, He has made us to be partakers of the glorious inheritance in eternity in paradise with the saints of light. And He has further delivered us from the power of darkness and already translated us into the kingdom of His dear Son. And for this, we certainly should be continually giving thanks to God; this is the principal reason for our gratitude.

"Thanksgiving encompasses the whole of the Christian life.... There are at least 140 references in Scripture to thanksgiving." (Richard Dinwiddie)

So I would ask you to consider your prayers. How many times do we rush into God's presence with this or that petition, this or that request, with little or no time for praise or for gratitude? So our wingless prayers barely make it to the ceiling of our room. We need those strong pinions of praise and thanksgiving if our prayers are going to be successful.

To change the metaphor, I think one of the reasons many people's prayers are not answered is that they're like plants in very acid soil—a soil unlikely to produce any sort of crop, a soil that's acid because it is filled with complaining and grumbling and thanklessness.

A major reason why people aren't grateful is that they suppose they deserve whatever they have. Why should they be grateful for what they deserve? I once saw a clip from the TV program *The Simpsons* that had something to do with Thanksgiving. In this scene, the father said that they were going to give thanks for the food, and the son replied something along these lines: "Why should we give thanks to God for the food? You worked and paid for it, Mom cooked it and served it, and I set the table. Why should we be thankful to God?"

That expresses the attitude of many people. Since they feel they deserve all they have in this life (and since, in the opinion of many, they actually deserve far more than they have), why should they be grateful? Of course, if they would stop and think a little bit, they would realize that there are many people who would be incapable of holding a job and making a living and buying their food. There are many thousands of such people in this country. There are other people who, though capable, live in parts of the world where a decent living is just not widely available, and so millions are living in poverty and hunger.

Are you thankful? Do you express gratitude to other people? I think of women who probably have heard very little in the way of gratitude from their husbands; I think of children who never satisfy their parents' demands and expectations and who never hear, "Well done, I'm happy to have you as a child, I'm proud of you and delighted with you"; I think of husbands who hear little or nothing in the way of gratitude from wives.

Another reason why gratitude is important is that it has a profound effect, we're told, on our health. You can't be grateful and really anxious at the same time. Doctors tell us that stress can cause many a disease. I believe a thankful heart and trust in a sovereign God who is going to work all things together for good can reduce the effects of stress in our lives. Therefore, we should be grateful.

When you're tempted to complain, look at Christ on the cross.

When you're tempted to grumble, contemplate the Crucifixion.

When you feel ungrateful about some sort of difficulty in your life, remember Him who endured the cross, despising its shame. Without this cross, we would have no access to God or any of the other blessings we enjoy, including those that have been highlighted in this book.

While we should thank the Lord regularly for our health, for our family, for our job—above all, we should thank Him for going to the cross.

---

*Prayer: God, grant us to form the good
habit of gratitude that flows consciously
from our minds, and may we learn
to stop, to think, and to give thanks.*

"How sharper than a serpent's tooth
it is to have a thankless child!"
(Shakespeare, *King Lear*)

✦

31

WORTHY
IS THE LAMB

*Worthy is the Lamb who was slain to receive power and riches
and wisdom, and strength and honor and glory and blessing.*

REVELATION 5:12

The great irony of Christianity is that at the cross, the devil
seemed to defeat Jesus Christ. But in truth, Jesus Christ, the
Lamb of God, defeated the devil at the cross.

You recall the awful time when Abraham was commanded
by God to take his son Isaac up to Mount Moriah and to offer
him there as a sacrifice. And so with broken heart, Abraham and
Isaac made this long trudge to the mountain. They began to
climb this mountain—Isaac with a bundle of sticks upon his
back for the sacrificial fire and Abraham with his broken heart
climbing afterward. But he went with hope, a hope that God
could even raise the dead, for He had promised Abraham that his
seed would be in Isaac.

At length Isaac asked this question: "My father!... Look, the
fire and the wood, but where is the lamb?" And Abraham, out of
his faith and hope, responded, "God will provide for Himself the
lamb" (Genesis 22:7–8). His answer was evidently a double
entendre, a double-meaning sentence. It meant that God Himself
would provide the lamb, but also it meant something deeper,
something even more profound. It meant God would provide
Himself as the Lamb. When Isaac was bound to the altar and
Abraham with knife in his hand was about to pierce it into his

son's heart, his hand was stayed by God, and there appeared a ram caught in the thicket for the sacrifice.

But that was a ram, not a lamb, and the question went unanswered. *Where is the Lamb?* That question echoed down through the halls of the entire Old Testament, and was repeated by the prophets. The blood of ten thousand times ten thousand animals killed upon the altars of Israel could not supply the Lamb who could take away sin and bring peace and forgiveness to the grieved and guilty hearts.

The ages passed, centuries went by, until at length, out of the wilderness there came a man with a leather girdle and clothing of camel's hair—the strange prophet John. Seeing Jesus in His white robes walking toward him, John uttered the final answer to that long-asked question: "Behold! The Lamb of God who takes away the sin of the world!" (John 1:29). At last the question was answered, and along with that answer, mankind was given a command: to *behold* this Lamb. To behold. *Nota bene* (note well; carefully observe). This is the Lamb of God, not the lamb of an individual or a household to take away the sin of a year or one nation. This is the "Lamb of God who takes away the sin of the world." God, indeed, had provided Himself as the Lamb, for this was God's only Son, who had come as the Lamb of God to die.

DID YOU KNOW?
Three times in the rest of the New Testament, Jesus is referred to as the Lamb, but in the book of Revelation, John refers to Him twenty-eight times as the Lamb of God.

To properly behold the Lamb, it is appropriate, I believe, that we turn to the book of Revelation. It is called the Revelation of Jesus Christ to Saint John, but perhaps it should be called the Book of the Lamb. Author Dr. Herbert Lockyer points out that Revelation "is essentially the Book of the Lamb. The entire volume revolves around Him. He is the center and circumference of this mystic and glowing book. It is also to be noted that Christ is always presented as the Lamb that was *slain*. The scepter of universal sovereignty will rest in His pierced hand. His cross wins Him the crown.... His wounds, evidence of His past sufferings." Here is a reminder of our present sin, and a reflection of the fact that there yet remains for those who are impenitent, a penalty to be paid.

An innocent, meek, and mild Lamb is the One we are to behold. We're told in the Book of the Lamb about the blood of this Lamb that makes us clean: "These are the ones who come out of the great tribulation, and washed their robes and made them white in the blood of the Lamb" (Revelation 7:14). We see that this Lamb has been slain and has shed His blood. That is the essential work of the sacrificial Lamb. For the Bible made it abundantly clear; it was incontrovertible. God said: "Without shedding of blood there is no remission" (Hebrews 9:22). In other words, God will not forgive sin without the shedding of blood.

Today, many people think that when they sin, they can simply pile a few more good works on the other side of the scales. They do not know they have no hope of ever being good enough—that the passing grade is not fifty-one percent, but one hundred percent.

We're all stained by sin. That stain cannot be removed by our doing good deeds. Without the shedding of blood, there is no remission of sin. Thankfully, the blood of the Lamb of God has been spilled and is all sufficient for those who trust in Him.

Prayer: Lamb of God, who takes away the sin of the world, take away our sin.

"Christianity without the Cross is nothing."
(James Thomson)

❧

32

IF GOD IS FOR US

If God is for us, who can be against us?

ROMANS 8:31

I f God is for us, who can be against us?" What a challenging question that is from the apostle Paul. He throws down the gauntlet to the whole ungodly world—to both men and demons. Who, indeed, could possibly be against those whom God is for? Surely, God plus one always equals a majority.

Paul dedicates the entire chapter of Romans 8 to building assurance within believers—an assurance of the fact that we are saved and safe and secure, both now and everlastingly. It's one of the most comforting and encouraging chapters to be found in Holy Writ.

In this particular portion of Romans 8, we find ourselves right in the midst of what we could call Paul's "Who's Who"—plus, to coin a phrase, Paul's "Whom's Whom," if we want to be more specific. As I was studying this passage I discovered four declarative *whom's* and four interrogative *who's*, and therein lies a fascinating story.

A most fascinating text is verse 29: "For whom He foreknew, He also predestined." What does "For whom He foreknew" mean? It means those God knew personally. This is the first link in what is known as the Golden Chain—a chain that stretches all the way from eternity, and is linked to the crystal palace in paradise. It's a Golden Chain which binds us to the love of Christ from eternity to eternity.

Take a look in this passage at these four *whoms*, which together refer to God's elect, to God's own, to God's peculiar people—to the redeemed, to the believer, to the saved:

For *whom* He foreknew, He also predestined to be conformed to the image of His Son, that He might be the firstborn among many brethren. Moreover *whom* He predestined, these He also called; *whom* He called, these He also justified; and *whom* He justified, these He also glorified. (vv. 29–30)

Notice that this last phrase doesn't say He glorified *some* of those He justified, or *most* of them, or *many* of them—but rather it is fully inclusive: *Whom* He justified, He glorified.

In the following verse, Paul goes on to say, "What then shall we say to these things?" (v. 31). What "things"? The things he has just iterated for us—the Golden Chain of the everlasting love of Christ. If God has so fixed His love upon us and has called us and justified us and will glorify us, what shall we say to these things?

Paul then adds this: "If God is for us, who can be against us?" (v. 31).

In the verses that follow,

"I will never need to be given over to the wrath of God's consuming fire because my Savior and Atoner was once given over to it, at Golgotha." (Bo Giertz)

we discover four interrogative *whos*, and in each case they refer to the nonelect, the unbeliever, the ungodly, the unsaved:

If God is for us, *who* can be against us?… *Who* shall bring a charge against God's elect?… *Who* is he who condemns?… *Who* shall separate us from the love of Christ? (vv. 31–35)

Amid these questions, Paul affirms the utter certainty of our salvation:

> He who did not spare His own Son, but delivered Him up for us all, how shall He not with Him also freely give us all things?... It is God who justifies.... It is Christ who died, and furthermore is also risen, who is even at the right hand of God, who also makes intercession for us. (v. 32–34)

Paul then conclusively affirms that absolutely nothing in all the universe or in all eternity "shall be able to separate us from the love of God which is in Christ Jesus our Lord" (v. 39).

What a glorious text this is. I hope you will revel in it, wallow in it, grasp the full implication of it. No one can be against you successfully. You cannot lose. Sometimes people are asked the question: What would you do in life if you couldn't possibly fail? We can't possibly fail to receive the love of Christ.

Paul is saying we need to get the knowledge of this love deep down into our souls. If God is for us—and if we trust in Christ, He most certainly *is* for us—then *who* can succeed in being against us? *No one.*

I've chosen to call this the "Golden Shield." It defends us from all the attacks of the evil one and his minions so that we're safe and secure forever.

Who can be against us? *No one.* The world, the flesh, and the devil—all fail.

My friend, may I remind you that all this centers on the cross of Jesus Christ? *There* is the focus of all the most important things in the world and the great benefits of the Atonement:

- It is the cross upon which His blood was shed for our sins.

- It was on the cross that His body was broken because of our transgressions.
- It is the cross from which the Golden Chain was made.
- It is the cross that makes up the Golden Shield.
- It is the cross that makes all of this a part of the Golden Grace of God, through which alone we are accepted and we rejoice in God and in His love and grace.

The cross is the key you insert into the lock on the door leading to heaven. It's the only key that fits. The cross was the gavel God used to declare us justified because sin had been punished in His own Son.

The cross, indeed, is the center of all things. He wants us to remember. He wants us to bask in His love.

Prayer: Lord Jesus, You have loved us before even the galaxies were formed. Help us to know that we are bound by Your Golden Chain of Grace to the everlasting throne of God.

"The cross is the only ladder high enough to touch heaven's threshold."
(George Dana Boardman)

33

ALIENS

At that time you were without Christ, being aliens from the commonwealth of Israel and strangers from the covenants of promise, having no hope and without God in the world.

EPHESIANS 2:12

A liens. What strange and exotic image does that word conjure up in your imagination? *Webster's* defines *alien* as a being of a different nature; aliens are beings who are incongruous and coldly, dispassionately unsympathetic to life in this world; they are strangers, foreigners, not owing allegiance and not partaking of the privileges of a state.

If you have traveled in a foreign land, you will know what it means to be an alien, to be in a real sense separate from the background and customs and language of the people. This is to be a stranger, to have people look at you as someone different— something alien.

We all are familiar with aliens. There are aliens in this country. We hear much about illegal aliens. The apostle Paul, however, tells us that an alien is precisely what each one of us at one time was, or perchance still is, in a far more significant sense than any of those I just mentioned. Each one of us has been an alien to the kingdom of God. Each of us was an alien to the commonwealth of Israel—a spiritual alien with a different nature. Each of us was excluded from privileges. Each of us was a stranger, a foreigner to the covenants of promise.

Paul says three things about these aliens: They are without Christ, without God, and without hope—a very doleful trinity of losses for anyone.

> As soon as we are at home in the kingdom of Christ, we become aliens in this world.

It's a somber thought to be without Christ and, therefore, to be alien from the things of Christ and the kingdom of Christ. Yet there are many such in this country, both outside and inside the church, out on the streets and even sitting in the pews.

How can you know if you're an alien to Christ? For one thing, you don't speak the language, you don't understand the customs, and you have a different nature.

Secondly, Paul gives another feature of the alien: He is godless. He is without God in the world. What a dreary picture to contemplate. You say, "Surely I have a God." Yet listen to what the Bible says: "Whoever denies the Son does not have the Father either" (1 John 2:23). If you don't have Christ, you don't have the Father. He who does not believe the Son does not believe the Father. You say, "Well, there are many ways to God. There are many people who worship God in different ways. All religions worship a god; they are not godless." But there's a major difference between the God who made the universe by merely speaking it into being and idols we've crafted with our hands or imagined up in our own minds.

The third condition of those who are aliens to the kingdom of God is that they are without hope. Ours is very much like the time in which Paul wrote these words: "having no hope and without God in the world"—ours is also an age without hope. When Paul wrote this passage, the Greek religions had faded away and the Roman religions were a mockery. People had indeed come to be without a god. It was preeminently the age of suicide. Many of the Caesars took their own lives. One of the common topics of conversation was what method one might use to dispatch oneself from the misery of this world. Tacitus, the Roman historian, tells us of one man who committed suicide simply out of indignation for having been born.

We, too, live in a day of suicide. Suicide is one of the most frequent causes of death among college students today. This is a tragic and sad condition brought about by the hopelessness arising from the godless teaching in many of our universities today. What a strange and sad plight for people to be in.

However, since we are in Christ Jesus, we're brought into the most intimate relationship with God. Christ is our High Priest, and we, in Him, come into the very presence of the Father, where we have communion with Him. We who were afar off have been brought near by the cross. We who were aliens have been made fellow citizens. This is our privilege. This is our joy.

Prayer: Father, we praise You that You have
sought us when we were aliens from the kingdom
of Christ and have drawn us in by Your Spirit
into Your kingdom of grace and beauty.

"Abandon all hope, you who enter." (Sign at the entrance of hell in Dante's *Inferno*)

34

CRUCIFIED
WITH CHRIST

I have been crucified with Christ: it is no longer I who live,
but Christ lives in me; and the life which I now live in the flesh I live
by faith in the Son of God, who loved me and gave Himself for me.

GALATIANS 2:20

There should be three crucifixions in the life and experience of the believer.

The first, and the one best known, is that Christ was crucified for each of us. "The Son of God…loved me and gave Himself for me," Paul says in Galatians 2:20. This crucifixion—the cross of Christ—was the heart of the preaching of the apostle Paul. The heart of his whole Christology was the fact that Jesus Christ came and gave Himself for us. "For I determined," Paul said, "not to know anything among you except Jesus Christ and Him crucified" (1 Corinthians 2:2).

He gave Himself for me—that's the first crucifixion.

The second crucifixion deals with our relationship to the world. In Galatians 6:14 Paul says, "God forbid that I should boast except in the cross of our Lord Jesus Christ, by whom *the world has been crucified to me*, and I to the world." So the second crucifixion is the fact that the world has been crucified to me—which is how we become aliens in this world.

I'm quite convinced there are many people in the church of Christ today who may have grasped the concept of the death of Christ and go about glibly declaring that Jesus died for them, and yet they don't even faintly perceive the fact that this also means the world is to be crucified to them.

When the New Testament speaks of the "world," it is not referring to the created universe, or to the stars and clouds and mountains and flowers, but rather, most always, to the world *system*. The Bible is talking about the corrupt system of this world—with all its evil devices, with all its vain and false and selfish and corrupt desires, its aims and goals and purposes, its self-centeredness and egotism. The "world" in Scripture is this whole corrupt system passed down from father to child through the centuries. The result of man's rebellion against God has been the establishment of a whole world system, which the Bible says is passing away.

"When Christ calls a man, he bids him come and die." (Dietrich Bonhoeffer)

The Bible says that if we are Christians, the world has been crucified to us, and it is therefore dead to us. It's somewhat like a man who greatly loves a woman, but one day she dies, perhaps even in his arms. He looks down at her body which just a moment ago was warm and moving. Now all is silent. The light has gone from the eyes. Perhaps, if he really loved her, he might even yet smother her face with his kisses. Wait but an hour or so and that body will grow cold, and a little longer and it will no longer be soft but now stiff and cold. Wait but a few days and it will begin to stink and rot. A week later, one would not be able to stand being in the room with it. That's what the Bible says should be happening in every believer's life concerning this whole world system, with all its vaunted success, all of its goals.

A woman said to me recently, "Have you reached your goals in life? Have you gotten out of life as much as you wanted to?"

I answered her, "Many years ago I stopped that struggle and ceased trying to get out of the world what I wanted. I realized that success isn't how much I can get from the world, but rather how much I can give to it."

For the third crucifixion in the life and experience of the believer, we go back again to Paul's words in Galatians 2:20, where he says, "*I have been crucified with Christ.*" Christ is crucified for us in substitution, but Paul goes deeper into the mystery that is Christ and says that if we want to understand the profound meaning of the cross, we will have to see not just substitution, but also *identification*. We will have to see not only Jesus dying in our place, but also *ourselves* on that cross dying with Jesus. If Jesus merely died instead of us, then Jesus will merely rise instead of us. The Scripture says we are *crucified with Christ* so that we may *rise with Christ*. If there is no identification in the cross, there will be no identification in the resurrection. This is part of the very essence of the theology of Paul.

Everyone would like to have an abundant life, and Jesus said, "I have come that they may have life, and that they may have it more abundantly" (John 10:10). But many people never seem to quite grasp *how* to have this abundant life. This is how: We live in proportion as we die. If you would have an abundant life, then what you must seek is an abundant *death* in Jesus Christ. That's always the law of the spiritual world. We rise by descending; we live by dying; we receive by giving. That is the law of the kingdom of God.

Jesus often said that if we lose our life we will find it, while those who find it will lose it. If you're seeking to hold on to your life, you're going to lose it; if you're willing to give it up, you'll find it. That means we need to seek for God to slay our old nature, which is keeping us from enjoying the abundant life Christ came to give us.

Prayer: O God, teach us to die to ourselves
that we may live for You.

Forbid it, Lord, that I should boast,
Save in the death of Christ, my God;
All the vain things that charm me most,
I sacrifice them to His blood. (Isaac Watts)

❧

35

THE GLORY
OF THE CROSS

*God forbid that I should glory, save in the cross
of our Lord Jesus Christ, by whom the world is
crucified unto me, and I unto the world.*

GALATIANS 6:14, KJV

We're so used to the cross that we've become numb to its horrors. The Roman populace thought of crucifixion as a cruel, inexorable, horrible punishment. Roman leaders agreed that the cross should never come near the person of a Roman, nor enter even his thoughts or eyes or ears; it was contemptible and to be used only on slaves and foreigners.

The Jews despised the cross as well. Paul declared, "Cursed is everyone who hangs on a tree" (Galatians 3:13), drawing those words from Deuteronomy 21:23 in the Jewish Scriptures. Though the Jews hated the cross, many of them hated Jesus even more as they cried out, "Let Him be crucified!" (Matthew 27:22–23).

This terrible, horrible, excruciating form of execution, which was the horror of the ancient world, became the glory of the apostle Paul, who declared, "God forbid that I should boast except in the cross of our Lord Jesus Christ" (Galatians 6:14).

We all glory or boast (it's the same word) in something. In what do *you* boast or glory? Is it the flowers in your front yard, or your score at the country club, or the new car in your driveway, or the old trophies on your mantelpiece? Perhaps it's the size of your bank account, or the size of your muscles, or maybe the style of clothes that cover your lack of muscles. Whatever it is, we all glory in something.

The Bible tells us there are some "whose glory is in their shame" (Philippians 3:19). I remember attending a hearing

---

DID YOU KNOW?
According to Dr. Edwin Yamauchi, professor at Miami University (Ohio), crucifixion was considered so horrible and degrading that it was not until centuries later, during the Byzantine period, that Christians began to artistically depict Christ on the cross.

---

before our local city commission when we succeeded in stopping the sale of alcohol at places that had erotic nude dancing. Listening to some of these dancers testify of the perfect propriety and nobleness of their profession, I thought to myself: *They glory in their shame.* There are also drunkards who glory in their drunkenness, and drug addicts who glory in their addiction. There are prostitutes who glory in prostitution and who carry signs down the street to prove it. There are fornicators who glory in their fornication, liars in their lies, adulterers in their adultery, homosexuals in their perversion, and blasphemers in their blasphemy. They glory in their shame. Yet the Scripture says their end is destruction: "For the wrath of God is revealed from heaven against all ungodliness and unrighteousness of men, who suppress the truth in unrighteousness" (Romans 1:18).

But there are, secondly, many more who glory in their supposed excellencies—their birth, race, nationality, education, position, accomplishments, wealth, power, talents, abilities, intelligence. But in all these things, I'm reminded of the Scripture that says: "And what do you have that you did not receive?" (1 Corinthians 4:7). Are you well-born? What did you have to do with it? Are you proud of your race or ethnic background? You ought not to be, but if you are, what did you have to do with it anyway? If you have a good education, who ultimately made it possible? Have you achieved a good position and great accomplishments? That's good, but even our talents, abilities, and intelligence are given to us by God. Not only that, but the very strength we use to draw upon and improve those gifts is also given to us.

One look at the cross of Christ convinced the apostle Paul of the emptiness and vanity of the world. He determined right then that in his ministry to people he would know nothing except Christ and Him crucified. He chose to glory in nothing except in the cross of our Lord Jesus Christ.

There's no doubt Paul could have had a great deal to glory about and to glory in, for prior to his conversion he was a Pharisee of Pharisees and very devout (Philippians 3:4–9). After his conversion, no one worked harder to share the gospel with the lost than the apostle Paul, and he suffered immensely for it. He even lists all the incredible persecutions he endured for the gospel's sake (2 Corinthians 11:23–28). But he gloried only in the cross of Christ.

What do you glory in? I guarantee you that whatever it is, it pales in comparison with the cross of Jesus Christ.

Prayer: Lord, help us to say with the apostle,
"God forbid that I should boast except in the
cross of our Lord Jesus Christ."

"It has been the cross which has revealed to good men that their good-ness has not been good enough." (Johann Hieronymous Schroeder)

CHRIST MY LIFE

For to me, to live is Christ, and to die is gain.

I can honestly say that Christ is the ordinary purpose of everything in my life—whether it be to get up or go to sleep, to exercise or to rest, to eat or to fast, to study or to work, or to do anything at all. The great overarching, transcendent purpose of everything I do is Christ. With Paul I can say, "For to me, to live is Christ." He is the purpose of my existence.

What is your purpose for life?

Dr. Louis Evans, formerly at the Hollywood Presbyterian Church in California, was invited to speak at a fraternity meeting one time. He went to the frat house and the students were sitting all around the room—on the floor, in the chairs, on the couch, on the arms of the furniture and everywhere. He was talking about purpose for life, and he asked one of the young men, "What is your purpose for living?"

The young man said, "Oh, I plan to become a lawyer."

He said, "Well, that's how you're going to make your living, but what are you living *for*?"

Another man said, "I want to have a wife and children."

And Evans said, "Those are the people you're going to be living with, but what are you living *for*?"

I would ask you the same question, my friend. What are you living for? You're going to get up tomorrow morning, and you're going to get dressed—for what? You may have to honestly admit:

"Because I keep waking up every morning." But is that all? Is there no more glorious reason for your existence?

Not only should Christ be the pattern and purpose of our lives, but He should also be the *passion* of our lives. There are very few people in the church, I'm afraid, who have a *passion* for Christ.

David Livingstone, the great missionary to Africa, who gave his life to reach unreached peoples with the gospel, declared, "I never made a sacrifice. We ought not to talk of 'sacrifice' when we remember the great sacrifice which He made who left His Father's throne on high to give Himself for us."

Years ago, I read a book about a young man who was passionate to spread the Good News of the cross. The name of the book is *Bruchko*. That's the closest the Motilone Indians of South America could come to pronouncing his actual name, "Bruce." It's a marvelous story about Bruce Olson, a young man from Minneapolis—a tall, gangling, angular, thin Swedish-American with a great crop of blond hair and blue eyes.

At around the age of twenty, he boarded a plane in Minneapolis and flew to Miami, and from there to Caracas, Venezuela. He had no training, no seminary education. He had shared the gospel with many in Minneapolis, but now he wanted to go where no man had gone before with the gospel—like the great apostle Paul, who brought the gospel to those who hadn't heard it before. So it was to the Motilone Indians in the depths of the jungles of South America that Olson was going.

Olson didn't know any Spanish, so he couldn't have known that *Motilone* came from the word meaning "mutilate." They were mutilating Indians, as anyone who had the great misfortune to ever find himself in those jungles discovered to his horror. Even the army of Venezuela dared not go to these jungles.

After a harrowing journey into the jungle, in which he

received an arrow through his leg, he finally reached the Indians. Instead of either killing or mutilating him, they simply dragged him to their village and left him in a heap. Eventually he recovered, and amazingly, some of the young people in the jungle came to believe in the message Bruchko came to bring them—the message of Christ. Then, after many months, Olson heard about the great chief of the Motilones who lived in another village about a nine-day walk away. The chief had heard how Bruchko had come into their jungle, and the chief said that as soon as he laid his eyes on him, he would kill him.

"I must go to see him at once," Olson said—because, you see, there beat within his chest the heartbeat of Christ.

The trek was dangerous, but Olson finally made it. Hearing of his coming, the chief came out with a poisoned arrow in his bow. He looked upon the strangest sight he had ever seen—this blond-haired, blue-eyed, utterly helpless creature. For some reason known only to God and him, the chief changed his mind and decided not to kill or mutilate him. That chief eventually accepted Christ, as did hundreds of others from the Motilone tribe all over the jungles of Venezuela—all because of a passionate young man who made living for Christ the purpose of his life.

When Christ is our life, it becomes our passion to know Him and make Him known. And when we finally see Him face-to-face, there will burst forth from your lips hallelujahs to Him who has conquered death once and for all.

Prayer: From now on everything is for Christ.
O God, by Your Spirit, make this true in our lives.

"What the sunshine is to the flower, the Lord Jesus Christ is to my soul." (Alfred Lord Tennyson)

37

THE GUILT IS GONE

He has...conveyed us into the kingdom of the
Son of His love, in whom we have redemption
through His blood, the forgiveness of sins.
COLOSSIANS 1:13–14

Dr. Karl Menninger, of the famed Menninger Clinic, relates the following fascinating story. On a sunny day in September 1972, on a street corner in the busy Chicago Loop, a plainly dressed, stern-faced man stood stiffly on the corner staring at the pedestrians flowing past him. Then he fixed his eye on one person close by, raised his hand, and with pointed finger said to him: "Guilty!" Then he lowered his hand and resumed his unmoving stance. After a few moments he repeated the gesture—again the inextricable raising of the arm, the pointing of the finger, the piercing fixed gaze, and the arresting word: "Guilty!"

Dr. Menninger said the effect of this strange pantomime upon the passersby was eerie, to say the least. They would stop, transfixed, and stare at their accuser for a moment. They would look down, look back at him, glance at one another, and then hurriedly make their way down the street. One of the men who was so accosted and arraigned said bewilderedly, "But how did he know?"

Guilty!

Sir Arthur Conan Doyle, creator of the famed fictitious detective Sherlock Holmes, was a practical joker. He once wrote a letter to a dozen or so of his friends who were prominent men of distinction in Great Britain. The unsigned note was confidential. There was no return address. These distinguished gentlemen each tore open their envelope, removed the note, and read these succinct words: "All is discovered. Flee at once." No signature. Within forty-eight hours, all of them had left the country.

Guilty!

A sense of guilt pervades our society. It has debilitating and disastrous effects upon human life. What are the effects of guilt?

One result is anxiety. Guilt creates a sense of anxious fear, a sense of angst—the unnamed fear that seems to hang over many people and causes them to want to look over their shoulder when they walk down the street. They feel that some nemesis, some goddess of vengeance is following after them and will wreak upon them the justice of the gods. This anxiety, and the ill effects produced by anxiety in the human heart, is the result of guilt.

The results of guilt also include depression, an inflamed conscience, a bad self-image, and physical illness.

And what really is this guilt that brings such hurtful consequences? I would venture to say that if you asked a hundred people what *guilt* means, ninety-nine of them would give a wrong answer. That's a very bold statement. Perhaps you feel you're the hundredth and will get it right.

What is guilt? Most everyone will say, "Guilt is the bad feeling you get when you've done something you know to be wrong." Wrong. That is *not* guilt. It's neither what the Bible means by guilt—which is the only real guilt—nor is it even what the law means by guilt. It's simply a definition of *guilt feelings*, and there's a great deal of difference between *guilt feelings* and *guilt*.

Suppose I placed my hand on a burner of a kitchen stove until I cooked several layers of flesh and created great blisters on my hand, and then someone asked me what a burn is. Would I be accurate by saying, "A burn is a searing feeling I get in my mind"? No, that is a burned "feeling," if you will. The burn itself is something very different and very real.

What is true guilt? According to the Bible and according to law, *guilt is the liability to punishment.*

Martin Luther said that the law is a mirror to show us our sin, a hammer to shatter our self-righteousness, and a whip that drives us to Christ.

Guilt is also permanent, as if it were engraved on granite. Semantical games won't get rid of it. Guilt can't be blame-shifted away, as many people try to do. This is called the "hot potato" game—just simply toss it to someone else, much like Adam tossed it to Eve, and Eve tossed it to Satan. We still do this today.

Often people try unsuccessfully to sublimate guilt or exchange it for some other emotion. People often try to substitute anger. For example, your wife asks you to go to the store to purchase a gallon of milk. You go to the store and buy the milk, then halfway home discover you left your wallet on the checkout counter. You return frantically to the store and find that it's gone. The clerk never saw it. You go home and tell your wife what happened, and before she can say one word, you get angry and say, "You and your milk!" You see, it's easier to feel angry than it is to feel guilty, so we shift the guilt to someone else.

Perhaps the most commonly mistaken idea of all about guilt is that time will simply wash it away. However, all the time in the universe won't diminish guilt one bit. It's like gravelly mud thrown against a plate glass window, where it hardens into a rocklike substance. Every time God looks into the window of the soul, He sees all the guilt. All the sin is still there, and time will never take it away.

A well-known hymn asks, "What can wash away my sin?" then gives this answer: "Nothing but the blood of Jesus." We read in Ephesians: "In Him we have redemption through His blood, the forgiveness of sins" (Ephesians 1:7). Scripture is explicit: "For the wages of sin is death" (Romans 6:23); "The soul who sins shall die" (Ezekiel 18:20); "Do not be deceived, God is not mocked; for whatever a man sows, that he will also reap" (Galatians 6:7).

The penalty for your guilt *will* be paid. The only hope we have is the hope that is found in Christ—and Him crucified.

Prayer: Father, forgive me and wash me
whiter than snow through Your Holy Spirit.
For Jesus' sake.

Jesus paid it all.
All to Him I owe;
Sin had left a crimson stain,
He washed it white as snow.
(Elvina M. Hall)

38

FORGIVE US
OUR DEBTS

Forgive us our debts, as we forgive our debtors.
MATTHEW 6:12

Not far from New York City there's a small cemetery wherein may be found a most unusual grave and headstone. There is no name on that headstone; there is no date of birth nor date of death; there is no epitaph, no fulsome eulogy; there is no embellishment of the sculptor's art. There is in fact but one word, one single solitary word, one all-encompassing word of three short syllables—the word *FORGIVEN*.

But that is the most important word that can be recorded about any human being who has ever walked upon the face of this earth, since it's true that the trail of the serpent has left its slime upon every human soul. And since it's true that sin is endemic in the human race—afflicting everyone from the pauper in his cottage to the king upon his throne—and since it's true that the Judge of all the earth has pronounced His verdict of "guilty as charged," forgiveness is critical. And since it's true that not one of us can endure the execution of this condemnation, the greatest need of all mankind is that we might receive forgiveness.

Consider another person. He had journeyed several hundred miles beyond civilization, into the far northern reaches of Canada. What misfortunes had befallen him we aren't told, but his journey had, at long last, come to its end. He was found seated in a small hut he had constructed, where his food had long ago run out. There was an inverted pie pan on his knees, which he had used for a writing desk. And in his skeleton hand was a letter he had been writing to his mother when death overtook him.

In this letter he said that it had been more than forty days since he had seen a human being and that it seemed there was no more blood left in him, since it had been so long since he had eaten. He said he could walk only a few steps now, and surely the end must soon come. He had a few magazines to read, but the stories in them now seemed so silly; he had a deck of cards, but playing solitaire seemed out of the question. He wrote that there was only one thought, one all-engrossing thought, one all-encompassing thought that filled his mind night and day: Would God forgive his sins?

Every sane creature who has lived his life beneath the gaze of the Almighty must surely ask himself that same question: Will God forgive my sins?

The cross provides the all-sufficient answer to this critical question.

The Apostles' Creed declares, "I believe in the forgiveness of sins." The great glory of the Christian faith is its affirmation of the forgiveness of sins.

> "As we are obligated to be sorry for our particular sins, so was He grieved for the sins of us all."
> (Matthew Henry)

Consider for a moment characteristics of God's forgiveness: God forgives fully and completely. He says, "For I will forgive their wickedness and will remember their sins no more" (Jeremiah 31:34, NIV). David writes, "As far as the east is from the west, so far has He removed our transgressions from us" (Psalm 103:12). And the prophet Micah acknowledges to the Lord, "You will cast all our sins into the depths of the sea" (Micah 7:19).

In decades past, one of the most active members of our

church went daily into the prisons to minister to inmates. He went regularly from the 1940s until he died in 1994. Charlie Hainline was phenomenal. He used to have prisoners memorize Bible verses as he led them to Christ and discipled them. One of the key verses he had them inscribe in their hearts was 1 John 1:9, which says, "If we confess our sins, He is faithful and just to forgive us our sins and to cleanse us from all unrighteousness." Charlie called this "the Christian's bar of soap." We're to use this daily. We're to go to the cross daily and receive forgiveness for our sins.

Not that we are to sin intentionally. Some people presume on the grace of God. They say, "If I sin, God will forgive me. After all, He's in the forgiveness business. So I may as well sin." This to me shows that they do not understand God's grace, or the cost of that grace. They're arrogantly presuming on grace. I doubt they truly know the Savior.

We need daily forgiveness for daily sin. But how can we be truly saved if we continually fall into sin? Contrast a pig and a lamb. When a pig falls in the mud, he stays there. When a lamb falls in the mud, he wants to get clean. When a truly regenerate person falls (and we all fall—some worse than others), he feels terrible about it and seeks (and finds) forgiveness—because of the cross of Jesus Christ.

Of course, we should do everything in our power to avoid the temptation. We should stay connected with trusted fellow believers who will hold us accountable. We should cut off everything within our power that will cause us to sin, and so on. Furthermore, there is such a thing as scandalous sin that would disqualify a Christian leader from uninterrupted service. But no sin is greater than the forgiveness found in the cross.

We do well to remember the thief on the cross beside Jesus—a thief who was guilty of capital crimes. He was receiving the due reward for his deeds, but he ended up receiving the gracious forgiveness of Christ. Jesus told him, "Today you will be with Me in Paradise" (Luke 23:43). And the glory of the Christian religion is the glory of its grace—that we may be forgiven by the grace of God, regardless of what we've done.

"Isn't that too easy?" some say. Well, it's easy for us to receive the forgiveness of Christ, but it wasn't easy for Christ to procure it. He was skewered to the cross in order to accomplish our forgiveness.

Prayer: Thank You, Jesus, that there is forgiveness to find at Your cross.

"Let us go to Calvary to learn how we may be forgiven. And let us linger there to learn how we may forgive." (Charles Spurgeon)

AS WE FORGIVE
OUR DEBTORS

When we are cursed, we bless; when we are persecuted,
we endure it; when we are slandered, we answer kindly.
1 CORINTHIANS 4:12–13, NIV

The Lord's Prayer teaches us that God will not only provide for our daily needs, but will also forgive us our debts as we forgive our debtors. The cross is always to be the source of our forgiveness, but the measure of it is as we forgive those who sin against us. And so when you get ready to ask God for the forgiveness of your sins, you might ask yourself this question: Is there anybody who has hurt me whom I haven't forgiven?

This request—"And forgive us our debts, as we forgive our debtors" (Matthew 6:12)—is the only petition in the Lord's Prayer where Christ afterward gives us a commentary on it. He adds a positive statement: "For if you forgive men their trespasses, your heavenly Father will also forgive you" (6:14). And a negative one: "But if you do not forgive men their trespasses, neither will your Father forgive your trespasses" (6:15).

I want you to know the importance of forgiveness. First of all, it's important even from a temporal and physical sense. We might first note, as physicians have said and as many books have been written about, that a failure to forgive can lead to heart failure and the failure of your life altogether. It causes devastating consequences in the physical bodies of men and women.

Doctors now know that ulcers are caused less by what we eat

than by what is eating us. So what is eating you today?

If you want to have a miserable existence physically and have a whole host of diseases, hold resentment and unforgiveness in your heart. It can destroy the body. You might as well drink a quart of carbolic acid.

A lack of forgiveness can totally destroy your personality. It can turn a sweet, happy, lovely young lady into a cold, hard, bitter woman. It can take a genial gentleman and turn him into a hard-boiled cynic who steps all over anyone who gets in his way.

> "Forgiveness does not leave the hatchet handle sticking out of the ground." (Anonymous)

Then there's the spiritual consequence—our own experience of God's forgiveness is intimately related to the forgiveness we grant to others. Suppose a millionaire forgave us a 10-million-dollar debt that we could never hope to repay, yet we turn around and hound someone else who owes us a mere one hundred. How would this millionaire feel when he heard about our pettiness? How can we honestly say we know the forgiveness of the Lord, if that's how we are in terms of not forgiving others? (I've just given you a modernized paraphrase of the parable of forgiveness found in Matthew 18.)

Forgiveness is at the core of Christianity. To truly forgive others we must humble ourselves, recognizing that Christ has forgiven us for a whole host of worse things.

Christianity is not primarily an ideology, a worldview, or a belief system. It is power. And forgiveness is the center from which the power is poured out. God steps in and creates something new; a new power enters our world and our lives. This power is the life in the kingdom of forgiveness. God forgives us our sins, first positionally in justification. He positions us in Christ and looks at us through Him as if we never had sinned. Then, relationally, He makes us His children and daily cleanses us from sin and the impurities of this world that cling so easily to us.

We know that God Himself will right all wrongs and that vengeance belongs to Him. Therefore we can say with Paul, "Being reviled, we bless" (1 Corinthians 4:12). Christians do not "look out for number one"; we give up our rights, and we speak well of those who speak evil of us. We give up our right to punish someone or to get even. Here lies the power of the gospel.

Forgiveness is divine. And because it is godlike, those who exhibit forgiveness stand out among men, like Mount Everest among the foothills. Without forgiveness, we will not make it in this life, nor will we make it to heaven. Unforgiveness and resentment will destroy the body—through ulcers or other diseases. It will destroy our spirit by making us cold, hard, and bitter. And it will destroy the soul.

To daily receive forgiveness from God, while daily forgiving others, is living the Christian life. The importance of forgiveness to our bodies, to our spirits (personality), and to our eternal souls could hardly be overemphasized.

Prayer: Father, forgive me for I have sinned of my own free will in what I have done and what I have failed to do. Lord, I release from my judgment anyone who has wronged me and forgive them by the power of the cross and the cleansing from Your blood.

"Forgiveness is the fragrance the violet sheds on the heel that crushed it." (Mark Twain)

40

"AS THE FATHER HAS SENT ME"

Peace to you! As the Father has sent Me, I also send you.
<small>JESUS, IN JOHN 20:21</small>

One of the key applications of the cross is that we want to spread the Good News of Christ's salvation. As the Father has sent the Son into the world, so the Son has sent us into the world.

Missions is not merely a matter of winning the lost. It is also God's way of distributing His inheritance. Missions is not something reserved for a few faithful folk; rather, every one of us is called to be a missionary. Jesus said to His disciples, "You shall be witnesses to Me in Jerusalem, and in all Judea and Samaria, and to the end of the earth" (Acts 1:8). Wherever we are, we're all to gather in the clan for that great feast in heaven.

May I remind you that the very few years and days we have on this earth are going to determine our everlasting inheritance? They'll determine where we will be forevermore in that day when God will divide His inheritance among His children. They'll determine the makeup and extent of our eternal reward.

Secondly, missions is not only God's way of distributing His inheritance; it is also God's way of maturing His children. God is a God who gives, and who is concerned about others. We who have lived through the "me" generation—the generation of self-fulfillment, self-actualization, and self-aggrandizement, always looking out for number one—find that we worship a God who is concerned for other people. We worship a Christ who wept over Jerusalem, who gave Himself unstintingly day and night to reach the lost, to help the poor, to heal the sick.

Most children generally tend to be very self-centered. They think the world revolves around them, with their parents meeting all their needs. And if somebody takes one of their toys, there's a howling that's heard down the block. There are many Christians who are just that self-preoccupied and self-centered. But we're called to give of ourselves—of our substance, time, and energy—in order to help other people. That's how we grow. Missions is God's way of maturing Christians.

DID YOU KNOW?

The contrast between the Sea of Galilee and the Dead Sea is most enlightening as an analogy to evangelism and the lack of it. Both receive water, but only the Sea of Galilee gives out water, which flows into the Jordan River. The Dead Sea, on the other hand, only receives water (from the Jordan), and has no outlet. It only takes, and never gives back. Consequently, it stagnates and is "dead." The same applies in our spiritual lives. Those who receive and give out, thrive; those who only receive and never give out, stagnate.

Thirdly, missions is God's way of reaching a lost world. You probably have heard the statement, "We are the only hands and feet God has, and the only mouth and lips He can use." Balderdash. What palpable nonsense is this? The Bible says: Can He who fashioned the ear not hear? Can He who made the mouth not speak? Can He who made us out of the clay of the earth not do anything He wishes? God can do anything He wants. No purpose of His can be restrained. He does what He wills "in the army of heaven, and among the inhabitants of the earth" (Daniel 4:35, KJV).

God can do anything He wants. He can even speak. He spoke to the people of Israel from Mt. Sinai. They heard His voice. Jesus spoke from heaven to Saul of Tarsus. God can do anything. God could easily have converted anybody He wanted by Himself, just as He converted Saul. He spoke to Saul. A light shone upon him. He fell from his horse onto the ground, and he was struck blind. His heart was changed and he became a new person. He became Paul the apostle (*apostle* means "one who is sent").

So it is actually a wondrous privilege that the Lord *invites* us to tell other people about the Good News of the cross. God could have done it Himself, or He could have sent angels—but instead He has left it to us poor men and women to do it. And what a great honor this is.

So why don't more Christians witness? There's a key reason why they don't. One leader of a Christian organization did a survey of thousands of Christians, asking them if they witnessed for Christ on any kind of regular basis, and if they didn't, why not? I thought the results were interesting. What do you think would be the number one reason given by thousands of people for not witnessing? That they hadn't been trained? That they hadn't been to seminary? That they were not knowledgeable enough about the Bible? That they were too busy?

No. Rather, this was their answer: "The life I live." They did not believe they lived the kind of life that was commensurate with the gospel.

May God help us live in a way that's consistent with and worthy of the cross. May God use us to make disciples, sharing the Good News of the cross by which we have received the forgiveness of sins.

Prayer: Father, we pray that today we will determine to win the lost to Christ through the power of Your Spirit.

"If God calls you to be a missionary, don't stoop to be a king."
(Jordan Grooms)

41

THE FIRST
LORD'S SUPPER

With fervent desire I have desired to eat this
Passover with you before I suffer.
JESUS, IN LUKE 22:15

On the night Jesus was betrayed—the night before His crucifixion, the night we call Maundy Thursday—what was
the first thing He said to His disciples when He sat down with
them? (We rarely ever put it all together to know what really took
place on that most significant night.)

The first thing He said to them was this: "With fervent desire
I have desired to eat this Passover with you" (Luke 22:15). This
form of speech is a Hebraism, which means, "With great desire I
have desired to eat this with you...with great longing I have
desired to do this."

I don't know who your heroes are in life. You probably know
some famous people—at least you know *about* them; you've

146

never met them, but you're sure they're just absolutely special people. You know you'll never meet them, and one thing is absolutely for certain: You're never going to have a meal with them. Even if you could ask them, they would no doubt turn you down.

But suppose you got an *invitation* from your hero for dinner? You would be floored. And when you sat down to dinner, suppose your hero said, "Eagerly I have desired to eat this meal with you."

I just express it this way that you might see something of the astounding nature of Christ's statement. The second Person of the Triune God, the Eternal Creator of the universe desires with great desire to eat this Passover with these all-too-human disciples of His.

How did they respond? Believe it or not, they started arguing among themselves as to who would be greater in the kingdom of God. Right there we see the incredible condescension and love of Christ in juxtaposition with this childish, selfish quarreling of the apostles as to who should be greater.

Christ's response? He took off His robe, girded Himself with a towel, poured water into a basin, and began to wash their feet. In what incredible contrast do we see the nature of sinful human beings and the nature of Christ! Though all the disciples were in shock, it was left to Peter to open his mouth (as he did so often and so often tragically):

Peter said to Him, "You shall never wash my feet!" Jesus answered him, "If I do not wash you, you have no part with Me." Simon Peter said to Him, "Lord, not my feet only, but also my hands and my head!" Jesus said to him, "He who is bathed needs only to wash his feet, but is completely clean; and you are clean, but not all of you." (John 13:8–10)

Having washed their feet, Jesus sat again at the table and made this astounding pronouncement: "One of you will betray Me.... He who dipped his hand with Me in the dish will betray Me" (Matthew 26:21, 23).

DID YOU KNOW?
The word *Eucharist* comes from the Greek *eucharisteo,* which means "I give thanks." Jesus took the cup in the very first Last Supper, and Mark tells us that He gave thanks for it (Mark 14:23). Christians have been giving thanks ever since, each time we participate in the Lord's Table.

They all began to inquire, "Lord, is it I? Lord, is it I?" They were astonished that such a thing as this could happen.

Judas Iscariot also asked, "Rabbi, is it I?" (Matthew 26:25). And Jesus answered him, "What you do, do quickly" (John 13:27). Judas went out, and even then the other disciples did not suspect he was going to betray Christ.

Then Jesus took bread, "and when He had given thanks, He broke it and said, 'Take, eat; this is My body which is broken for you; do this in remembrance of Me'" (1 Corinthians 11:24). Then we read: "Then He took the cup, and gave thanks, and gave it to them, saying, 'Drink from it, all of you. For this is My blood of the new covenant, which is shed for many for the remission of sins'" (Matthew 26:27–28).

Having distributed the cup and the bread, Jesus began what is considered to be the most intense and deepest discourse in all of Scripture. It's found in chapters 14–16 of the Gospel of John, and it begins with these words:

Let not your heart be troubled; you believe in God, believe also in Me. In My Father's house are many mansions; if it were not so, I would have told you. I go to prepare a place for you. And if I go and prepare a place for you, I will come again and receive you to Myself; that where I am, there you may be also. And where I go you know, and the way you know. (John 14:1–4)

And over this great affirmation there is a response of doubt on the part of Thomas: "Lord, we do not know where You are going, and how can we know the way?" (14:5).

Jesus answered, "I am the way, the truth, and the life. No one comes to the Father except through Me" (14:6).

After this great discourse, they went out. Scholars think that on the way to Gethsemane, Jesus prayed the real Lord's prayer—not the one that He taught the disciples, but the one He Himself prayed. This prayer is found in chapter 17 of the Gospel of John, and begins with these words: "Father, the hour has come" (v. 1).

The Lord's Supper has become a perpetual reminder of the cross of Christ. It will last until time ends, and then it will no longer be necessary.

Prayer: Help us, Lord, to never neglect
Your holy table, nor to ever let it
become mere custom.

"There is an inevitable similarity between the celebration of the Passover as a feast of the old covenant and the Lord's Supper as a feast of the new." (Dr. Walter Elwell)

42

THE MONUMENT
OF CHRIST

Do this in remembrance of Me.
JESUS, IN 1 CORINTHIANS 11:24

Some people have built great memorials for themselves to perpetuate their memories. For example, many of us may have seen in person the great pyramid at Giza, the greatest of all the pyramids in Egypt—a mammoth structure, the base of which is larger than a four city-block square. It's an enormous building. Herodotus, the Greek historian, says it took 400,000 men working day and night for twenty years to build it. I'm not sure about the numbers, but it was a gigantic undertaking. It was built as the Pharaoh's tomb so he would be remembered forever—great pharaoh that he was. You, of course, remember him. That was Pharaoh...ah...Pharaoh...ah...what?

His name was Khufu. Now, you remembered that, didn't you?

Probably not. My, did he go to a lot of trouble for nothing.

Then there was a fellow who built the largest structure ever built by mankind on this planet, allegedly the only man-made structure that can be seen from the moon. It's the Great Wall of China, and it was laid out and constructed for 1,500 miles across the Chinese frontier—a gigantic enterprise, ensuring its builder's enduring fame.

The wall, of course, was built by the well-known and famous...somebody help me. Who was it? Surely, we remember him.

Oh, yes—Shihuangdi (Shih-Huang-Ti). You knew that, didn't you? Was it just on the tip of your tongue?

Probably not.

Well, maybe it's not size that counts. Perhaps it's beauty. What is the most beautiful building ever built? Many experts agree that it's the Taj Mahal in northern India. It was built by Shah Jahan for his beautiful wife, who had died in childbirth. She would be remembered forever by the most magnificent, beautiful, gorgeous building ever built on this planet. I'm sure none of us will ever forget her. Her name was, uh…? What was her name again?

Her name was Arjumand. And you probably didn't know that one either.

In the second century, the apostles' teaching was summarized in a classic document called the *Didache* (which means "teaching"). From that document, here is a statement on communion: "On the Lord's own day come together, break bread, and give thanks, but first confess your transgressions so that your offering may be pure."

It seems that such great monuments as these are not likely to produce any real lasting remembrance or significance. Perhaps you're one of those who believes in immortality, as far as the memory of your family is concerned, if not the human race. But I wonder if you can even remember the first and last name of your maternal great-grandmother—your mother's mother's mother? (I venture to guess you don't; I can't remember the name of mine either.)

But let's consider Christ. What is His lasting monument? Is it the ruins we find in the Holy Land, where He left His footprints two thousand years ago? Is it the great cathedrals of Europe? Is it the Vatican, as some would say? One could argue that these things point to the monument Christ left behind. But I would argue the real monument of Christ is more subtle than these things.

The real monument Christ has left is not a gigantic pyramid of huge stones, but a living supper. These simple things—the bread and the cup—will yet last as long as time will last, continuing to speak. "For as often as you eat this bread and drink this cup, you proclaim the Lord's death till He comes" (1 Corinthians 11:26).

When the pyramids at Giza and China's Great Wall and the Taj Mahal have all melted away, the Lord's Supper will still stand. It's the great picture of what Christ came into this world to do.

In the simple reminder of the bread and the wine, we have a permanent monument of Christ. He gave His body for us and shed His blood.

When Christ was nailed to that cross, lifted up naked before all the world to see, enduring the shame and the horror and the agony and the pain of the worse kind of human suffering that could be endured, He hung there for three interminable hours until at last there came high noon. And then, in the peak of that day's heat, suddenly the sun's light failed, a great darkness descended at noon, and a blackness covered the earth. And there in that darkness, unseen by mortal eyes, there came a hand down from heaven and extended before His face that cup containing the sin of the world. It was placed to His lips, and willingly Jesus drank it down to the dregs.

The Scriptures tell us that Jesus Christ, the Holy One of God who knew no sin, *became* sin for us (2 Corinthians 5:21). During those hours, He endured God's wrath; God, His Father, who loved Him with an infinite and eternal love, dumped over the cauldron of His wrath toward sin on Jesus. He did it "that we might become the righteousness of God in Him" (2 Corinthians 5:21).

God loves us with an infinite love, but God hates sin with an infinite hatred, and that hatred fell upon His own Son. And at last, when it seemed an eternity had passed, Jesus cried, "It is finished!" *Tetelestai*—it was done; the price was paid; the debt was paid in full.

This is what we remember when we participate in the "monument of Christ," the great sacrament of the Lord's Supper.

Prayer: Lord, help us never to forget You and Your sacrifice. Thank You for the perpetual reminder that we can hold in our hands and eat.

"My beloved brethren, it is no temporal feast that we come to, but an eternal, heavenly feast." (Athanasius)

THE MYSTICAL UNION

Because I live, you will live also.
JESUS, IN JOHN 14:19

The Lord's Supper is one of the two great sacraments of the church (the other being baptism). A sacrament is a means of grace. But what does the Last Supper means to us today? What grace does it bring us?

As Christ's ministry of teaching and healing was completed, the hour for which He came into the world arrived—the hour of His suffering and death. In His lengthy prayer of John 17, Jesus prayed that He and we may be one even as He and the Father are one—that we might be united in Him. John Calvin calls this the most important of all the doctrines of salvation. It's what theologians call "the mystical union," whereby we and Christ are united. Christ comes into our lives and our hearts and unites His nature with ours, and we become one.

It's a mystery no one can fully fathom, but it is the clear teaching of Scripture. We're taught in the Bible: Christ in me, I in Christ, Christ in us, the hope of glory.

That's why when we participate in the Lord's Supper, we're not simply remembering a departed Friend who loved us even unto the end and gave Himself upon the cruel cross; nor are we merely looking forward to that time when He shall come again ("Do this until I come"). Rather, it's as if Jesus is saying: "Remember Me in the past, in the future…and *in the present as well*."

I recall many years ago reading a popular booklet entitled *My Heart, Christ's Home*. In it, the author describes the heart as a home with various rooms—living room, workshop, study, and others. He describes how Christ should richly dwell in each of those rooms and how His will should determine the nature of what goes on in every one.

He tells about Christ coming into a man's heart, and that man shows Him around all the various rooms of his "house." The Lord notices a library off to the left at the bottom of the stairs, and He says to this man, "Here, we can meet each morning and commune together as I share the great truths I want you to know and the love I have for you, and I can help you and strengthen you and guide you in your way."

So each morning this man comes down the stairs and eagerly turns into the library. There is Christ waiting for him, and the man shares with Him in prayer and in the Word and the fellowship of Christ. It's a wonderful time.

> Jesus, the very thought of Thee
> With sweetness fills my breast....
> The love of Jesus, what it is,
> None but His loved ones know.
> (Bernard of Clairvaux)

But there comes a day when the man's schedule is particularly hectic. He wakes up a little late and will barely make it to work on time, so he rushes down the stairs and out the door. The next day a similar thing happens, and the next. Soon he has forgotten all about the daily appointment in the library.

Months go by…one, two, three months. One day, on a particularly dark morning, he's coming down the stairs, and he notices light streaming from under the door in the library. He opens it curiously to see who might be there. To his amazement, there stands Christ. The man asks, "Lord, what are You doing here?"

Christ says, "Have you forgotten our appointment, that I was to meet you here every morning to share My love and My Word with you, and to help you and guide you in your life?"

"Oh—I'd forgotten about that, Lord. But…but, You haven't

been here every morning waiting for me, have you?"

"Yes…yes, I have." And Jesus added, "With fervent desire I have desired to have this communion with you"—words that echoed His greeting to His disciples (in Luke 22:15) on the night of His Last Supper.

To make sure we don't forget Christ and the incredible price He paid on the cross, Jesus instituted the Lord's Table, where we consume the elements in a permanent memorial. We experience His real presence in the Lord's Supper.

He said, "Do this in remembrance of Me." What are we to remember? *Him.* This isn't to say His teaching and His doctrine are not important, but they are not the foundation of our hope of everlasting life. Christianity is *Christ.*

Remember Him in His temptation.

Remember Him in His vilification, as He was continually being falsely judged and charged with all sorts of evils. He was called a wine-bibber and a glutton. He was called Beelzebub, the prince of demons. He was called an impostor and a fraud. Remember this One who had false witnesses come whose lies were believed so that He was condemned.

Remember Him in His crucifixion, where He endured the penalty of death we deserve—where His hands and feet were pierced, His body was broken, His blood was shed.

Remember Him in His abandonment, as God the Father abandoned His beloved Son.

Remember Him as He took our guilt upon Himself and endured the wrath of God in our place.

Remember Him.

Dear friend, all of this was endured for you and me. How can we ever thank Him enough?

"What wonder then if a love so great is expressed in a common feast." (Tertullian)

Prayer: Lord, help us to never forget Your cross and never forsake Your Table.

44

MEDITATIONS ON COMMUNION FROM A DYING PASTOR

The Lord Jesus on the same night in which He was
betrayed took bread; and when He had given thanks,
He broke it and said, "Take, eat; this is My body which
is broken for you; do this in remembrance of Me."
1 CORINTHIANS 11:23–24

Modern evangelicalism seems a bit happy-go-lucky. If you were to read the New Testament, you wouldn't necessarily find the positive health-and-wealth gospel proclaimed from some pulpits today as being derived from the Gospels and the Epistles.

What a contrast to those messages do we find in the deep insights of a pastor dying of cancer a century and a half ago. Adolphe Monod, a French Calvinist pastor who lived from 1802 to 1856 and ministered in a church in Paris, delivered a series of messages as the cancer was slowly claiming his life. These sermons comprise the chapters of the book with a new translation by Constance K. Walker—*Living in the Hope of Glory.*

It would appear that each sermon is a communion sermon. As cancer was eating him from within, Monod took great comfort and found spiritual nourishment in feeding on the Lord's Table. He called it "the Lord's love feast," and he participated in it regularly.

We do not have an adequate view of sin, Monod asserts. Because of that, we misunderstand so much. Monod reminds his hearers that the cross alone is our source for the remission of sins. We're so saturated with sins in this world that we can't see how depraved we are.

We have no clue of how *evil* sin really is before a holy God. Maybe the closest we come is by looking at the cross.

All our suffering is deserved. We don't think so because we don't see the true degree of our sin. We don't suffer on behalf of others. Only Jesus did that. Our thoughts of sin should drive us to the cross.

What was available to Moses and to Abraham is available to us, through faith. Monod reminds us of Martin Luther's line about Satan: "One little word shall fell him." God isn't like a vending machine. We put in our dollar prayer and we get the answer. No, "the good things of God are not so cheap." It's easy to say words in prayer—but do we really mean them? Do we hunger and thirst spiritually? A day may come when we might not even have the strength to pray. We should not wait till then—not when faith can be found now. Following Christ includes in the desert, in Gethsemane, at the cross. We prepare to do His will tomorrow by doing His will today.

Monod says (citing an unnamed church father): "We have in the Old Testament *God for us*, in the Gospels *God with us*, and in Acts and Epistles *God in us*."

The sacrifice of Jesus is, of course, based on His suffering. We need to die to ourselves. Christ's death allows us to do that. Monod views his own sufferings as something that "God has had grace to visit on me." What a privilege it is, he writes, to be chosen by God to suffer so that his sufferings can comfort others.

Monod has such a winning attitude toward life. He cannot lose, come what may. Even his suffering is a privilege. He reminds us that when Christ appeared, it was not as a "man of joy," but of sorrows.

Suffering for the Christian is a winning proposition—it helps conform us to the image of Christ. Jesus' suffering served a great purpose—the salvation of souls. Only Christ atoned for sins in His suffering. But when we suffer, it can be of help to our brothers and sisters in Christ. Suffering is a privilege for the Christian because it can remind us of Him.

"We all suffer," Monod observes. Everyone suffers—if you're a thinking person. I'm reminded of a line from the movie *The Princess Bride*, which I paraphrase: "Life is pain. Anyone who tells you otherwise is trying to sell you something." To desire to be happy is perfectly legitimate; God gave us that feeling. But sin has disturbed what *should be*. There's no true consolation anywhere but the Scriptures.

> "[Christ] will never deprive me of any good except to give me some other, better one." (Adolphe Monod)

For the apostle Paul, both life and death are good. What a positive approach to life. Death is desirable in itself because we go to be with Him. Monod says, "Let us not distance ourselves from that which reminds us of [death]." Our modern culture has virtually perfected that. We hide reminders of death wherever we can—even using euphemisms such as "he passed away" or "he's gone" instead of "he died." Life to the Christian is win-win. Life is good; death is good.

Monod regrets having wasted time on some "minor matters"—not great matters. When a Christian is focused on *petty* things, this causes terrible harm. Monod makes a good distinction—focusing on *little things* is okay, but being consumed by petty matters is wrong. Christ always had His head in heaven while His feet were on earth.

God weighs true greatness. The purpose of living is to glorify

God. Unfortunately, too many of us are preoccupied with the wrong pursuits—riches, love of glory, selfish ambition. We should be breathing in the atmosphere of heaven. Sometimes it takes death staring us in the face to remind us of how, in the cross, God has solved the big issues of life.

Prayer: Lord, thank You for
the rich blessings we enjoy,
thanks to Your cross.

"Having Christ we have all things."
(Adolphe Monod)

45

JESUS VERSUS THE OTHER GODS

I am the way, the truth, and the life.
No one comes to the Father except through Me.
JESUS CHRIST, IN JOHN 14:6

A few years ago, one of my church members asked me about a course he'd taken in college on comparative religion. The professor said he had examined the teachings of Christianity, Buddhism, Confucianism, Hinduism, Mohammedanism, and all the rest, and concluded there essentially is no difference between them. They're all basically the same.

But the professor is wrong. Christianity is unlike all the others because it is not based upon the teachings of its Founder. It is based upon Christ Himself and Him crucified.

For instance, Lao-tzu, the founder of Daoism (Taoism), said, "Here is the way. Walk ye in it." But Jesus said, "I am the way. No one comes to the Father except through *Me*." Christ built His entire religion not upon His teachings, though they were the greatest teachings the world has ever seen, but upon Himself.

Consider this tale. A certain man fell into a pit that was ten feet deep and twenty feet square. In this filthy pit was a gigantic venomous serpent with glistening scales, black beady eyes, and a searching tongue.

The man was terrified. He tried to leap out of the pit, but he couldn't come close to the ledge above him. Meanwhile he strove desperately to stay out of reach of the serpent's deadly strike.

Then, on the ground above him, a stranger came alongside the pit. The man down below was delighted to see someone, and he called out, "Help me!"

Now it so happened that this stranger was a Buddhist. And if you know anything about Buddhism, you know that Gautama—who became Buddha, the enlightened one—once sat down under a tree for a number of days meditating, and during this time he was "enlightened." He discovered the answer to the question, "Why are people unhappy?" He had seen how miserable people were, and now he finally discovered the reason: People are unhappy because they want things they can't get. They are miserable because they don't have the things they wished to have. Therefore the cure for this problem must be that we should slay our passions, our desires, our wanting. Once we've killed all these longings to possess what we do not possess, we will then be happy.

DID YOU KNOW?
All other religions have nothing really to offer except teachings. Christ offers Himself. What fallen man needs is not a sermon, but a Savior. Buddha sat under the bo tree seeking illumination. Jesus hung upon a cruel tree, shedding His blood, to pay for our sins. Christ and only Christ is the Savior of the world. There are many religions, many prophets, many teachers, but there is only one Savior: Jesus Christ.

And so this Buddhist stranger looked down into the serpent's pit and said to the man he saw there, "Ah, my friend, I see that you're miserable. Do you know why you're miserable? You're miserable because you want to get out of the pit. You wish to be away from that serpent. You desire to be someplace far away. Now, sit down, fold your legs, lotus fashion, close fingertips, and think, *I am perfectly happy. I do not wish to be anywhere else. I'm not afraid of serpents. All is well. All is well. Ommmmmmm. Ommmmm. Ommmmm.*" And the Buddhist man left.

Meanwhile the man in the pit saw that the serpent was trying to get closer. He leaped to the other side of the pit, almost delirious with fear.

Then, on the ground above him, another stranger walked by, and the man in the pit screamed out to him for help.

This second stranger happened to be a Hindu. Now, if you understand anything about the beliefs of Hinduism, you'll know that Hinduism's essential truth is that the material world has no reality, no substance. It is maya. It's an illusion. The only thing real is Brahman, the spirit god, and therefore the essence of Hinduism's belief is simply that everything in this world is only an illusion with no reality.

And the Hindu said to the man in the pit, "Dear sir, I see that you have a problem. You're in a pit, and there's a serpent. Now let me see if I can enlighten you. You must understand that there is no pit; there is no serpent. There is no you. All is well." And he goes on his way.

Then along came a third stranger, and this man was a Confucianist. Now Confucius was also a wise man. He spent his time trying to teach people how they can be wiser in their lives, and he taught many good things. But as far as heaven was concerned or salvation or God, he said he knew nothing. But he did know how to tell this man to be wiser, and he said, "Ah so, a man fall into deep pit. Very unwise. Not good to fall in pit with serpent.

But this will be grand experience of learning for you. You'll learn from this that a wise man watches where he steps, and a wise man does not fall into a pit with serpent. Henceforth I guarantee that you'll never fall into a pit again."

Finally—Jesus came alongside the pit and saw the man and the serpent. He leaped down into the pit, placed His body between the man and the serpent, lifted the man up, and threw him up onto the safety of the surface above. At that same moment, the serpent sank its fangs into His heel and emptied the venom into His body. The man escaped—while Jesus died.

Prayer: Dear Lord, help us not to be
deceived by the many counterfeits out there.
Help us to cling only to Your cross.

"The world has many religions;
it has but one Gospel."
(George Owens)

46

ONE MEDIATOR

For there is one God and one Mediator
between God and men, the Man Christ Jesus.
1 TIMOTHY 2:5

I once was talking to a woman who was an outspoken oppo-
nent of Christianity, and somehow the conversation got
around to religion. I took out my New Testament and opened it
to the words of Jesus in one of the most familiar and beloved passages in the Scripture.

> "Let not your heart be troubled; you believe in God,
> believe also in Me. In My Father's house are many
> mansions; if it were not so, I would have told you.
> I go to prepare a place for you." (John 14:1–2)

Then I pointed to another verse on that page and asked her
to read it. It's where Jesus speaks these words:

> "I am the way, the truth, and the life. No one comes to
> the Father except through Me." (John 14:6)

The woman responded, "I just can't stand that kind of talk—
it's bigoted and narrow-minded, and I just can't stand it!"

I answered, "I know you can't stand it, but I just wanted
you to realize that it's Christ who made that statement—so
your argument is with Him. If you can't stand people who
make such statements, it's because you can't stand Christ."

The Bible explicitly declares, "There is no other name under heaven given among men by which we must be saved" (Acts 4:12)—no other name but Jesus.

The Bible also says, "He who does not honor the Son does not honor the Father" (John 5:23). There is no one honoring Christ who is not honoring God, according to the Bible. There is no one who knows or worships the Son who does not also know and worship the true God.

Why is that the case? It's true first of all because of who Christ is. He is *God*. He is the Creator of the world. He is the One who was before all things. He is the One before whom every knee shall bow. He is God Almighty, the second Person of the eternal Triune Godhead.

Yes, He is *God*—and just as He said that one day He would come to earth, so indeed He came.

When you think about it, there can be only one mediator between God and man. There are no other candidates for the job. No other religious teacher could possibly be a mediator between God and man because of the requirements involved in the job. By definition, a mediator is one who reconciles offended parties to one another. In doing this, he removes the obstacles in the path of reconciliation. Only Christ could, and did, do that. Only Christ dealt with the one obstacle that separates human beings from God. That obstacle is sin—nothing else.

Alfred Lord Tennyson described Jesus this way, showing how He bridges both heaven and earth: "The Lord from Heaven, Born of a village girl, carpenter's son, Wonderful, Prince of Peace, the mighty God."

God cannot abide sin. He is of purer eyes than to even look upon iniquity, and for any iniquity to come into His presence must mean that it will be instantly annihilated. Who has dealt with sin besides Christ?

What can take away our sin? Nothing but the blood of Jesus. There's nothing else that's even offered to take away sin.

We have seen throughout this book how Christ came to take upon Himself the guilt of our iniquity. It was imputed unto Him and laid upon His soul. Christ bore in His own body our transgressions. And God the Father punished sin in His own Son that we might be spared. Only in this way was the obstacle removed that stood in the way of reconciliation between God and man. That's why there can be no other mediator.

Not only would Satan try to deceive us about other "saviors" or other so-called mediators, but the devil would also have us set forth ourselves as our own savior. As man exerts his own will and demands to be his own lord and master, so he would try to be his own savior as well.

This is why there can be only one mediator. If we say all religions are alike, we're saying that Christ's atoning work is for naught.

The apostle Paul says that if righteousness could come by the law—if by following rules we could become righteous—"then Christ died in vain" (Galatians 2:21).

All the teachers from other religions are saying, in effect, "Follow me, and you will become righteous." Though we had the Ten Commandments for fourteen hundred years before Christ came, Jesus said, "Did not Moses give you the law, yet none of you keeps the law?" (John 7:19).

There is only one way to salvation, and that is in Christ.

By one offering of Himself upon the cross, Christ forever put away sin.

By one offering, He perfected forever those who will come to God by Him.

By one offering, He made it possible for us to come to God with a full assurance of faith.

By one offering, He gave us the absolute guarantee of heaven for those who will receive Him and trust in Him alone.

By one offering, He gave us the full forgiveness of sin.

This one Mediator is Prophet (who tells us the Word of God), Priest (who offered Himself as the sacrifice), and King. He is the great King of kings and Lord of lords.

The word *kingdom* comes from the two terms "king" and "dominion"—king's dominion. It exists wherever the dominion of Christ rules and holds sway over the hearts of men. Christ is the great King right now, ruling all things for the well-being of His church and bringing to absolute perfection and completion the plans for us which He ordained before the foundation of the earth. He is the King eternal and invincible. One day He shall return in glory and reveal Himself as the great conquering King, and then all shall know.

Prayer: Heavenly Father, thank You for giving us
Your Spirit by whom we know Your Son,
the one and only Mediator between You and us.

"Without Christ life is as the
twilight with dark night ahead."
(Philip Schaff)

47

A MATTER OF PROFIT AND LOSS

*For what will it profit a man if he gains
the whole world, and loses his own soul?*

JESUS, IN MARK 8:36

Charlemagne, Charles the Magnificent, was one of the greatest monarchs of the Middle Ages. He ruled over major portions of Europe. His wealth was infinite, his power almost without limit. As death approached, his distinct faith in Jesus Christ as his Savior caused him to plan a most unusual funeral for himself. His body lay in state in the magnificent cathedral at Aix-la-Chapelle, under the huge dome, dressed in his royal robes and seated on a magnificent throne gilded with gold and precious jewels. The royal crown rested on his head, and on his lap lay an open Bible, the forefinger of his right hand pointing at the words: "For what will it profit a man if he gains the whole world, and loses his own soul?"

Though long dead, Charlemagne may yet speak to the culture of America today, for the lesson he was trying to teach is one that most Americans haven't yet learned. There are no pockets in a shroud. We cannot take our wealth with us.

Try to imagine the following absurd scenario: The President of the United States has a six-year-old son who comes to his father and says, "Daddy, I would like to set up a lemonade stand in front of the White House."

His father encourages him, saying "All right, son, go right ahead."

Late that afternoon the little boy comes back into his father's office, all wide-eyed and excited. He says, "Daddy, Daddy, guess what? I made $1.23 today!"

"Oh," responds the President, with unusual interest, "That's wonderful, son."

The next day the father goes out to observe his son's lemonade stand, and he's struck by the fact that, indeed, business is brisk. In fact, on the second day the boy makes twice as much money as he did the day before.

By the third day, the father offers to help his son, and so the President of the United States could be found out on the street cutting lemons in half and squeezing them to make the lemonade.

He continued to help his son. By the second week, he was out there from morning until night. His staff, of course, were almost ready to pull out their hair. They said to him, "Mr. President, do you realize there are four ambassadors waiting to see you, two treaties that need to be signed, and the budget must be presented to Congress? Don't you understand?"

The President replies, "But don't you see, we made $12.40 yesterday? Business is growing at a phenomenal rate. Why, at the end of the year, I compute that we'll have made more than $32,000!"

Amazingly, there are some reading these words who are actually more foolish than this man was.

Each of us is engaged in various types of enterprises. On the one hand are those enterprises in which our bodies are involved— our flesh and bones and our senses, whether insignificant or of far greater pith and moment. For most people these take up the majority, if not all, of our time, energy, thoughts, and concern. Then there are the enterprises that are, by their very nature, eternal and infinite in scope. I refer to the enterprises of our soul.

The President of the United States was not elected by the people to run a lemonade stand. And you were not created by an eternal God to wallow in the mud flats of materialism. God has called us to far greater and higher things. "For what will it profit a man if he gains the whole world, and loses his own soul?" (Mark 8:36).

Jim Elliot, the famous missionary to South American Indians, put it so well in his diary: "He is no fool who gives up that which he cannot keep in order to gain that which he cannot lose." The reverse of that is the very height of folly. What will a man give in exchange for his soul?

> The death of an unbeliever can be unpleasant. Cesare Borgia, son of Pope Alexander VI, was a great prince. In fact, he is immortalized as a royal personification in Machiavelli's *The Prince*. He was devious and consummately dexterous in dealing with men and affairs. He was prepared for every extremity, for every circumstance of life. However, shortly before his death in a beseiged castle in 1507, he is said to have written, "I have provided in the course of my life for everything except death. Now, alas, I am to die almost entirely unprepared."

If you look around at our world today, you would suppose that our souls are of little value. Looking at television, you might be convinced man has no soul at all, or that its concerns are far beneath the attention of any intelligent man. When did you last see anyone on television demonstrate any concern for his eternal soul? We're bombarded on all sides by propaganda saying that our souls are of no value, and that only the things of this world are of surpassing importance. Therefore, we should give our complete attention to them.

Recently, an enterprising young man offered his soul for sale on eBay. In his view, he would gain financially from something he apparently didn't even think he had.

All of these things would conspire to say that Jesus is wrong when He surveys the whole of humanity and all human endeavors and says to us, "What will it profit a man if he gains the whole world, and loses his own soul?" Thankfully, because Jesus went to the cross, He has provided salvation for our souls.

Prayer: Oh, God, please show us the
folly of getting too settled here on earth and
planning only for things down here.
Please give us an eternal perspective on life.

"I am going into eternity,
and it is sweet for me to
think of eternity."
(missionary David Brainerd)

48

DEATH DEFEATED

And whoever lives and believes in Me shall never die.
Do you believe this?

Jesus, in John 11:26

The cross of Jesus Christ would be incomplete without His resurrection. When He rose from the grave, He conquered death once and for all. Therefore, death is defeated by the cross and by Christ's resurrection.

The great Dr. Samuel Johnson, who gave us the first magnificent dictionary of the English language and who was the center of social life in eighteenth-century London, once observed that most of us run from one vocation or avocation to another throughout our lives, all in a vain effort to avoid thinking about our mortality. Yes, there are many who may pretend they have no fear of death, but unless they've come to know the Conqueror of death, they're merely pretending and deceiving themselves.

Two thousand years ago, the Greek philosopher Epicurus observed that men feared not that death is annihilation, but that it is not.

Much more recently, the poet T. S. Eliot, in *Murder in the Cathedral*, declared: "Not what we call death, but what beyond death is not death, we fear, we fear." How true that is, and it has been echoed by numerous people, great and mighty.

Death means one thing to the Christian and something entirely different to those who don't believe.

Samuel Johnson, whom I mentioned above, wrote these

The great author Thomas Carlyle, when describing the phantas-
magorical scene that surrounded the funeral of Louis the
Magnificent—including swelling organ music that seemed to
be some plaintive prayer of hopelessness—said this: "Frightful
to all men is death, from of old named the King of Terrors."

words to a friend in the latter part of his own life: "Oh! My
friend, the approach of death is dreadful. I'm afraid to think on
that which I know I cannot avoid. It is vain to look round and
round for that help which cannot be had." Here was a brilliant
conversationalist, author, writer, intellectual—standing terrified
before death.

Sir Walter Raleigh may have described it best as he apostro-
phized death by saying, "O eloquent, just, and mighty Death!
whom none could advise, thou hast persuaded; what none hath
dared, thou hast done; and whom all the world hath flattered,
thou only hast cast out of the world and despised: thou hast
drawn together all the far stretched greatness, all the pride, cruelty
and ambition of man, and covered it all over with these two nar-
row words, *Hic jacet* ["Here lies"]!

Let us look at the dying words of some notable unbelievers
down through history:

Ernest Hemingway: "There is no remedy for anything in
life…death is a sovereign remedy for all misfortunes."

The Earl of Beaconsfield: "Youth is a mistake, manhood a
struggle, old age a regret."

Voltaire: "Son, choose your [Christian] mother's way, not
mine; she has chosen the better part."

Eugene O'Neill: "Life's only meaning is death."

H. L. Mencken: "What the meaning of life may be, I do not
know; I incline to believe it has none."

Matthew Prior: "He alone is blessed who ne'er was born."

Robert Ingersoll: "If there be a God, let him have mercy on my soul."

Friedrich Nietzsche: "If man has a why for his life he can bear with almost any how."

W. E. Lecky: Death is "the melancholy anticlimax to life."

What a contrast we see when we consider the dying words of Christians. For example:

D. L. Moody: "Earth recedes, heaven opens before me!"

John Wesley: "The best of all is, God is with us. Farewell! Farewell!"

Francis of Assisi: "Be praised, Lord, for our Sister Bodily Death, from whom no man can escape.... Blessed are they who are found in Thy holy will, for the second death will not work them harm."

If you trust Christ, you can know that when you leave this world, you're going to a realm where death cannot enter. You're entering

...a city that has no cemetery.

...a city decked with silver and lilies.

...a city where we will live forever with Christ.

...a city where there are transparent mansions of gold.

...a city through whose windows the lank-jawed skull of death cannot grin.

...a city where death's bony finger cannot beckon.

...a city where, in new and deathless bodies that shall glory in the thrill of endless life, we shall adore His matchless name.

That is what I desire for you—the certainty, the assurance, the joy which only Christ can give—and which comes when you realize you will soon be in that place where

...you will be rejoined to those you have loved and lost.

...you will receive all that has been taken from you in this life.

...you will indeed be crowned with the crest of triumph.

...you will look upon Him who is the Conqueror of death and the Lord of Glory, and you will stand full in the undimmed blaze of Immanuel's smile.

You will have reached paradise. You'll know that in this glorious place where the fountains are filled with the water of life eternal, you will look upon Him on His glorious Conqueror's throne and you will sing, "Hallelujah! Hosanna! Our Savior has conquered the tomb. Our Savior has conquered death. Our Savior has brought us all the way to glory."

---

*Prayer: Lord Jesus Christ, You alone
have conquered death. Thank You for the
sure hope of eternal life in Your presence.*

"Through his resurrection
he...set up a banner of victory
throughout all ages for his
saints and believers..."
(Ignatius)

BEAUTY AND THE BEAST

See what kind of love the Father has given to us,
that we should be called children of God; and so we are.
1 JOHN 3:1, ESV

Behold what manner of love the Father has bestowed on us, that we should be called children of God! Therefore the world does not know us because it did not know Him.

In the opening of this book, we mentioned how fairy tales often tell an aspect of the gospel. So many of them involve marriage between a noble prince and a princess who has been marred, but the prince loved her anyway. Jesus is that Prince. We are the restored bride, made beautiful by His love.

Take the same tale, only reverse the gender. You'll recall the story of *Beauty and the Beast*, where a beautiful young lady meets someone who was more beast than man—with a snout rather than a nose and hoofs rather than hands.

At first she was terrified. However, she came to realize that he was gentle, and not only gentle, but loving and kind. He was gracious to her. He began to bring her gifts, to tell her wondrous things. Finally she fell in love with the beast. One day, after the curse was lifted because of her unconditional love for him, he instantly turned into a handsome prince—which is what he had been originally before the curse.

We are like that beast—under the curse of sin, but transformed by the unconditional love of the Savior.

The gospel story has generated many secular kinds of stories, but in *Beauty and the Beast*, they got it upside down. The truth of the matter is that there was a handsome prince who went out into the woods and met a female beast who looked horrible, and yet He extended His love to her. He poured out His love upon her, and one day He kissed her right on her snout—and she turned into a beautiful princess.

We are that princess bride. Christ is Beauty—and wonder of wonders, He loves us in spite of all our ugliness, whether physical or spiritual. And because of His love, we are restored. That is the story of the gospel.

Jesus Christ is the true Prince, and He left the glories of His Father's house in order to seek and to save we who are lost. He has promised to redeem all those who believe in Him. We are now His heavenly bride, and we anticipate His marriage feast.

We noted at the start of this book that the Bible begins with a wedding and ends with a different wedding. Even the middle book of the Bible, the Song of Songs, is essentially a wedding book.

We should also note that there are some important trees found in the beginning, middle, and end of the Bible. In the Garden of Eden, we find the tree of life, from which humankind was banished. God drove these human beings (after their sin) out of the Garden, lest they eat from the tree of life. But in the last chapter of the Bible, the redeemed of God are permitted to eat from the tree of life.

Why? Because of the true tree of life found earlier in the New Testament—the "tree" upon which the Savior died. The cross of Jesus Christ is the true tree of life that gives life to all those who believe.

If you ever wonder if God loves you…

If the circumstances of life overwhelm you and you ever doubt the love of God…

If you know in your head "God loves you," but you don't feel it in the heart…

Then look to the cross. See Jesus Christ dying and suffering for you. Then see Him risen from the dead and ascended to heaven and seated at the right hand of His Father. Soon, He will return to gather His redeemed.

Even so, come quickly, Lord Jesus.

Amen.

Soli Deo Gloria

ACKNOWLEDGMENTS

Many thanks are due for the production of this book. First of all, we must thank our book agent, Bill Jensen, who originally conceived the idea and brought it to our attention. From start to finish, Bill skillfully helped make this book a reality.

Also, I must thank my incredibly dedicated and thoroughly competent secretary, Mary Anne Bunker. Her help is invaluable. Also thanks go out to Joanne Kahlke, substitute secretary, and to Nancy Britt, who helps edit virtually all our material.

Kirsti S. Newcombe played a critical role as a sounding board for these meditations. She too helped with the editing and rewriting.

We are also most grateful to the staff at Multnomah for their professional approach to the whole project. In particular, we thank Thomas Womack.

Finally…we can never thank Jesus Christ enough for going to the cross on our behalf. Everything we do for Him, including this book, is just a small token of thanksgiving for what He did for us on Calvary. As someone once put it, "His darkest day has become our brightest." Amen.

QUOTATION SOURCES

Chapter 1
Ken Hemphill, *The Prayer of Jesus* (Nashville: Broadman & Holman, 2001), 77.

Chapter 2
Thomas Adams, quoted in Frank S. Mead, ed., *The Encyclopedia of Religious Quotations* (Old Tappan, NJ: Fleming H. Revell, 1965), 200.

Chapter 3
Augustus M. Toplady, "Rock of Ages" (1776).

Chapter 4
Blaise Pascal, *The Mind on Fire: Writings of Blaise Pascal* (Portland, OR: Multnomah Press, 1989), 41–42.
Fanny Crosby, "Blessed Assurance" (1873).

Chapter 5
Charlie Hainline, as based on the remembrance of coauthor Jerry Newcombe. Charlie was an active lay evangelist at Coral Ridge Presbyterian Church in Ft. Lauderdale until his death in 1994. See more of his story in chapter 38.

Chapter 6
John Calvin, *Institutes of the Christian Religion* (Grand Rapids, MI: Wm. B. Eerdmans Publishing Co., 1997), 307.
Charles Spurgeon, *The Quotable Spurgeon* (Wheaton, IL: Harold Shaw Publishers, 1990), 103.

Chapter 7
Frederick M. Lehman, "The Love of God" (1917: lyrics based on the Jewish poem *Haddamut*, written in Aramaic in 1050 by Meir Ben Isaac Nehorai).
Justin Martyr, "Letter to Diognetus," quoted in Eberhard Arnold, ed., *The Early Christians: In Their Own Words* (Farmington, PA: The Plough Publishing House, 1970/1997), 297.

Chapter 8
C. S. Lewis, *Mere Christianity* (New York: Macmillan Publishing Company, 1960), 109.

Chapter 9
Justin Martyr, "First Apology," 52, quoted in Eberhard Arnold, ed., *The Early Christians: In Their Own Words* (Farmington, PA: The Plough Publishing House, 1970 / 1997), 150.
Lee Strobel, *Inside the Mind of Unchurched Harry and Mary: How to Reach Friends and Family Who Avoid God and the Church* (Grand Rapids, MI: Zondervan, 1993), 36.

Chapter 10

The New-England Primer (Boston: Edward Draper, 1777), 11.

Chapter 11

Paul L. Maier, professor of ancient history at Western Michigan University, as quoted in the D. James Kennedy video presentation *Who Is This Jesus?* (Ft. Lauderdale: Coral Ridge Ministries-TV, 2000).

Chapter 12

Paul L. Maier, as quoted in *Who Is This Jesus?*

Chapter 13

Justin Martyr, "Dialogue with Trypho the Jew" 111.1,2 in Arnold, *The Early Christians*, 150.

Chapter 14

Origen, "Homilies on Numbers" (xxiv.I), in Henry Bettenson, ed. and trans., *The Early Christian Fathers: A Selection from the Writings of the Fathers from St. Clement of Rome to St. Athanasius* (London: Oxford University Press, 1956/1978), 221.

Chapter 15

Jonathan Edwards, quoted in Mead, *The Encyclopedia of Religious Quotations*, 201.

Chapter 16

Arnold, *The Early Christians*, 176.

Chapter 17

Cicero, as quoted in Jurgen Moltmann, *The Crucified God* (Minneapolis, MN: Augsburg, 1993), 34.

Charles Clayton Morrison, quoted in Mead, *The Encyclopedia of Religious Quotations*, 395.

Chapter 18

Charles Wesley, "And Can It Be?" in *Psalms and Hymns* (1738).

Richard Hooker, quoted by Tim Keller, Redeemer Presbyterian Church, New York City, November 23, 1997, p.m. service.

Chapter 19

Augustine, trans. by John K. Ryan, *The Confessions of St. Augustine* (Garden City, NY: Image Books, a division of Doubleday, 1960), Book 10, Chapter 43, 274.

C. S. Lewis, *Mere Christianity* (New York: Macmillan Publishing Company, 1960), 154.

Chapter 20

Earle Stevens, quoted in Eleanor Doan, *Speakers Sourcebook II* (Grand Rapids, MI: Zondervan, 1968), 74.

Chapter 21

Justin Martyr, "Letter to Diognetus," in Arnold, *The Early Christians*, 297.

Chapter 22

C. S. Lewis quoted in Wayne Martindale and Jerry Root, eds., *The Quotable C. S. Lewis* (Wheaton, IL: Tyndale House Publishers, Inc., 1989), 62.

Chapter 23

Jerry Newcombe interviewed Dr. Alan Whanger in Ft. Lauderdale, FL in 2006 for a program on the Miracle Channel (Saransdal, Norway: www.miraclechannel.com).

Mary and Alan Whanger, *The Shroud of Turin: An Adventure of Discovery* (Franklin, TN: Providence House, 1998).

William R. Featherston, "My Jesus, I Love Thee" (1864: at 16 years old).

Ian Wilson, quoted in David Van Biema, "Science and the Shroud," *Time* (April, 1998), 57.

Chapter 24

Whanger, *The Shroud of Turin.*

Pierre Barbet, MD, *A Doctor at Calvary: The Passion of Our Lord Jesus Christ as Described by a Surgeon,* translated by the Earl of Wicklow (New York: P. J. Kenedy & Sons, 1953), 166.

Chapter 25

Acts of Andrew (Andrew's Death) in Arnold, *The Early Christians,* 300.

Chapter 26

Justin Martyr, "Dialogue with Trypho the Jew" 49.8; 52.4 in Arnold, *The Early Christians,* 148.

Chapter 27

Augustine, *Confessions,* Book 8, Chapter 7, 194.

Chapter 28

Henry M. Edmonds, quoted in Mead, *The Encyclopedia of Religious Quotations,* 132.

Chapter 29

Tacitus, in study notes for "The Crucifixion of Christ—John 19:18–30" (San Antonio, TX: Bible Study Fellowship, International, 2002), 1.

Napoleon Bonaparte, Philip Schaff, and H. G. Wells, quoted in Larry Chapman, ed., *Y-Jesus* (Great Falls, Montana: Y-zine, 2006), 96–97.

Chapter 30

Richard Dinwiddie, "The Sacrifice of Praise," *Christianity Today,* 20 November 1981, 40.

William Shakespeare, *The Tragedy of King Lear,* Act I, in Frank W. Cady and Van H. Cartmell, *Shakespeare Arranged for Modern Reading* (New York: Doubleday & Company, Inc., 1946), 951.

Chapter 31

James Thomson, quoted in Mead, *The Encyclopedia of Religious Quotations,* 95.

Chapter 32

Bo Giertz (Swedish theologian), Å Tro På Kristus (To Believe in Christ), translated by Kirsti Sæbø Newcombe (Oslo, Norway: Luther Forlag, 1973), 213.

George Dana Boardman, quoted in Mead, The Encyclopedia of Religious Quotations, 93.

Chapter 33

Dante, The Divine Comedy, quoted in The Oxford Dictionary of Quotations, 3rd ed. (Oxford et al: Oxford University Press, 1980), 171.

Chapter 34

Dietrich Bonhoeffer, The Cost of Discipleship (New York: Macmillan, 1963; translated by R. H. Fuller from the German Nachfolge, first published 1937 by Chr. Kaiser Verlag Munchen), 7.

Isaac Watts, "When I Survey the Wondrous Cross," in Hymns and Spiritual Songs (1707).

Chapter 35

Johann Hieronymous Schroeder, quoted in Mead, The Encyclopedia of Religious Quotations, 94.

Chapter 36

David Livingstone, quoted in Mead, The Encyclopedia of Religious Quotations, 391.

Alfred Lord Tennyson, quoted in Doan, Speakers Sourcebook II (Grand Rapids, MI: Zondervan, 1968), 74.

Chapter 37

Elvina M. Hall, "I Hear the Savior Say" (1865).

Chapter 38

Matthew Henry, Commentary on the Whole Bible, ed. by Leslie F. Church (Grand Rapids, MI: Regency Reference Library, Zondervan Publishing House, 1960), 1342.

Charles Spurgeon, My Sermon Notes (Grand Rapids, MI: Christian Classics, 1884), 264.

Chapter 39

"Forgiveness does not leave the hatchet handle..." quoted in Doan, Speakers Sourcebook II, 164.

Mark Twain, quoted in Mead, The Encyclopedia of Religious Quotations, 150.

Chapter 40

Jordan Grooms, quoted in Mead, The Encyclopedia of Religious Quotations, 308.

Chapter 41

Walter A. Elwell, gen. ed., Baker Encyclopedia of the Bible Vol. 2 (Grand Rapids, MI: Baker Book House, 1986), 1352.

Chapter 42
Didache, quoted in Arnold, *The Early Christians*, 203.

Athanasius, quoted in Bettenson, *The Early Christian Fathers*, 298.

Chapter 43
Bernard of Clairvaux, "Jesus, the Very Thought of Thee" (12th century: translated from Latin to English by Edward Caswall, *Lyra Catholica*, 1849).

Tertullian, quoted in Bettenson, *The Early Christian Fathers*, 142.

Chapter 44
Adolphe Monod, *Living in the Hope of Glory,* Constance K. Walker, trans. (Phillipsburg, NJ: Presbyterian & Reformed, 1856/2002), 161, 86, 87, 56, 100, 61, 48, 47.

Chapter 45
George Owens, quoted in Mead, *The Encyclopedia of Religious Quotations*, 308.

Chapter 46
Alfred Lord Tennyson, quoted in Mead, *The Encyclopedia of Religious Quotations*, 59.

Philip Schaff, quoted in Mead, *The Encyclopedia of Religious Quotations*, 58.

Chapter 47
David Brainerd, as quoted in Ron Rhodes, *The Undiscovered Country* (Eugene, OR: Harvest House, 1996), 32.

Chapter 48
T. S. Eliot, *Murder in the Cathedral* (New York: Harcourt Brace & Company, 1935); 72.

Walter Raleigh, *Historie of the World* (1614), book V, part I, chapter VI.

Thomas Carlyle, *The French Revolution: A History* (1837), Book 1, chapter 1.1.IV.

Ernest Hemingway, The Earl of Beaconsfield, Voltaire, Eugene O'Neill, H. L. Mencken, Matthew Prior, Robert Ingersoll, and Friedrich Nietzsche—quoted in Herbert Lee Williams, *A Man You Can Trust* (Memphis: Kirbilee Books, 1977), 111.

W. E. Lecky, quoted in Robert Ervin Hough, *The Christian After Death* (Chicago: Moody Press, 1974), 9.

D. L. Moody, quoted in Rhodes, *The Undiscovered Country,* 69.

John Wesley, quoted in Rhodes, *The Undiscovered Country,* 32.

Francis of Assisi, quoted in Will Durant, *The Age of Faith,* Volume IV of *The Story of Civilization* (New York: Simon & Schuster, 1950), 801.

Ignatius, "Letter to the Smyrnaeans," quoted in Arnold, *The Early Christians*, 216–217.

INDEX